As I exhale, a lightness comes over me and
I am extended into a space outside of guilt and
pain. A warm glow bathes over me.
I ask for another.

Bare

Lorna Tucker

brazen

March 2025
First edition

First published in Great Britain in 2025 by Brazen, an imprint of
Octopus Publishing Group Ltd
Carmelite House
50 Victoria Embankment
London EC4Y 0DZ
www.octopusbooks.co.uk

An Hachette UK Company
www.hachette.co.uk

The authorized representative in the EEA is Hachette Ireland, 8 Castlecourt
Centre, Dublin 15, D15 XTP3, Ireland (email: info@hbgi.ie)

ISBN 978-1-91424-073-7

A CIP catalogue record for this book is available from the British Library.

Typeset in 10.5/16.25pt Swift LT Std by Jouve (UK), Milton Keynes

Printed and bound in Great Britain.

10 9 8 7 6 5 4 3 2 1

This FSC® label means that materials used
for the product have been responsibly sourced.

To my children, for teaching me what true love is,
and my husband, for holding me when I could not stand

I have lived in Watford. I have lived in Camden. I have lived on many streets, in many pitches deep in the shadows within the stiking and filthy parts of Soho in London. I have lived in hostels as a single mum. I have lived all over London and many cities around the world. I have lived with almost every boyfriend I have ever had. I have lived with and without a daughter. I have lived with an abuser. Then I finally lived with a man who looked after me when I had two more children. Now I live alone with all of my children. The only thing I can tell you today, is that *I, Lorna Tucker, have lived.*

I am an addict. This is something that I must always remember, remind myself of each morning when I wake up. There is a history of addiction that runs through my blood.

The insanity of how the mind works when you are gripped by this . . . this what I can only describe as a disease . . . is madness, and chaos. Nothing really makes sense, but when you are living it, whatever drug you choose becomes all that matters.

It comes before absolutely *everything.* But you don't realise it's taking over, because that devil on your shoulder is very convincing, and tells you that everything is justifiable: I don't use that iPod anymore, I might as well sell it;

we never watch TV, I should sell it as it's just sitting there; my daughter never wears these shoes anyway . . .

I'm ashamed of so much. The shame I carry from my past, there is so much that has held me back from living for so long.

I don't want to be ashamed anymore.

This is my story. All the truth I can remember. Nothing but the truth. Please don't judge me, God (but I don't believe in you anyway).

1

Generic pebble-dashed housing estate, Watford.
Mid-1980s.

I am standing against the wooden bannister on the upstairs landing. I'm around five or six and it's post-sibling communal bath time. My white damp nightie clings to my lower legs. The rest of the family are downstairs. The sound of a game show peels through the open crack of the living room door. I wobble on the precipice of the stair ledge but manage to steady myself. My stomach feels strange – to get rid of the shame lodged inside I realise I have to jump. I peer down at the drop below. It's ten or so stairs. I don't see a way round it. So I close my eyes, stretch out my arms and step forward. And it all stops. Time stops. I just hang there. I look around. I am floating.

I've always taken things too far. Been 'too much'. Spun myself round and round until I nearly passed out, held my breath under water until I felt light-headed and detached from the world, jumped off staircases to realign my mind. Then it became drinking till I would pass out or be sick. Smoking weed till I couldn't see straight. Taking pills till I couldn't think straight. Shooting up till I couldn't live straight.

My parents weren't bad people. An aerial view of the living room when I was born would show my doting mother lying on the sofa breastfeeding me, my brother playing with plastic figurines on the floor, my dad coming back from a long day at work. A house. A home. And two loving parents, that's more than most. Still, it was bad at times. But it was also good. They met by chance at the Hopbine, a fifties' nightclub. My dad fell in love with my mum the moment he set eyes on her. They dated for a while, married and soon she was pregnant with my brother. She told me once that up until the doctors examined her she still believed that babies were born out of your bum.

Just before I arrived my parents were living in a caravan in a trailer park by the motorway in Watford, a suburb just north of London. My mum was staying home all day struggling with my then two-year-old brother and trying to navigate the cramped living conditions with her ever-expanding belly. The floor was sagging and rotten. They moved into a council flat not long before I was born, but, of course, I don't remember any of that.

By the time my mind could hold on to any memory we had moved again, to a three-bedroom council house in Watford. The house that was to become the backdrop to my youth. You see, my mum was a resilient woman, she had experienced a lifetime of hardship and constantly wanted to better her life.

She gave to us the best start in life she could, but had no role model on how to parent. Her dad was an alcoholic and died from cirrhosis of the liver, and her mum was forced to undergo electric shock treatment due to depression.

My mum was four and her sister 18 months when they were placed in a children's home. Over three years later, my nan collected them and introduced them to their new stepfather before leaving him and relocating to Spain, where she started to drink heavily, leaving them to run feral. Through their teens, my mum and her sister worked in hotels, saving up every penny to escape back to England. But soon after they arrived back, her sister disappeared after a night out, never to be seen again. My mum had lived through neglect and abuse. She had tried her hardest to break this pattern, but she had been broken. She had us to find a reason to live, maybe.

My dad had come from a more stable and settled home environment, two loving parents who stuck together. He liked to fix up cars outside the front of his house, and paint in his spare time. As the youngest of three boys, my dad, the softest of the three and a near-seven-foot gentle giant, was the only man in the family who didn't join the military. Instead he followed in his dad's, and grandad's, post-army tradition of working at the Kodak factory in Harrow, developing photos. He always had a camera round his neck.

When I was four years old my dad moved out and started living at my grandma's around the corner from us. Later, a stranger started coming to visit for tea. I could sense there was something different to her other friends by the way my mum my acted around him. My brother and I would visit my dad on the weekends; he'd take us to fast-food restaurants for burgers and fries and we'd play free and wild. Eventually he got remarried and our visits with him became less and less frequent.

One day, my mum announced my nan was coming to visit. I'd never met my mum's mum as she lived in Spain. When I asked Mum where her dad was, realising she must have had one too, all she said was,

'He's dead.'

A few hours later my dad pulled up with our nan in his car.

My brother and I learned pretty quickly that she didn't like children, and would give you a whack over the back of the head or on your butt with a slipper, wooden spoon or coat hanger if you didn't do as she asked. We were used to Mum screaming at us out of frustration, but not this kind of violence.

As Mum spent more time with the stranger I missed our family time together and felt jealous of the attention she gave him. She was *my* mum. I just wanted to cuddle with her and my brother on the living room's sagging sofa.

I knew that we had lost part of her to him, and that things would never be the same again.

One night, the stranger carried her through the front door, which I found funny, before he came back with more boxes and suitcases full of his things. Not long after, the mysterious grumpy old woman left.

At first the stranger bought us gifts, swung us about and took us out on late-night adventures, stealing sweetcorn from the local fields, however it was fleeting as his violent behaviour towards my mum soon began. And as time unfolded we saw another side to him.

Soon things really started to fall apart. Mum was tired all the time. She seemed sad all the time too.

One morning my brother and I were playing with a homemade slingshot and accidentally hit a Champagne flute, displayed on a top shelf in the lounge. We knew it spelt trouble as soon as the shatter rang throughout the house, we held our breath and hid behind the lounge's open door. Silence. Then, all at once, the stranger's big hairy arm appeared, pulling my brother from safety. I watched helplessly through the door crack as he slapped my brother. They left my line of sight and I could hear the sound of my brother being dragged upstairs to our bedroom. I wanted to run after them, to help him. To make the stranger go away. But I felt trapped behind the door.

On another occasion my brother was smacked and sent to bed without any dinner for being cheeky to the stranger. We tiptoed around the house and tried our very best not to upset this man with long hair who stomped around our house in muddy boots and wore wax jackets. He kept handguns in the cupboard that he would get out on Sundays to clean, and pet ferrets in the garden for hunting.

'If they bite you, they will never let go,' he'd say as he placed them next to us on the sofa.

He would go hunting on Sundays, with big, sharp, steel-jawed traps and the ferrets, and would come back by 6pm with dead rabbits and pheasants on strings, which he would give to my mum to skin and cook.

The kitchen where she skinned his hunted animals also became the place where he hunted her too. I would hear her screams as he persecuted her. She tried to hide his violence towards her. But often I could hear my mother struggling to breathe next door.

Memories charge into my mind of seeing the stranger's hands around her throat as he is pushing her against the fridge, spitting as he speaks.

'I'd rather kill you before letting you leave.'

My mum's eyes, full of fear, freeze on me.

I hid under the table more and more: hiding from the debt collectors, hiding from the stranger when I did something wrong, from the sound of plates smashing.

The more they fought, the more I retreated into myself under that table.

After fifteen months and countless hours under that table, Mum finally managed to get rid of him. The stranger left and never came back.

2

One Sunday afternoon when I was 11, I sat next to my granny drinking her Blue Nun. We were watching a soap where one of the female lead characters tried to kill herself by swallowing a packet of aspirin. The idea that I was able to end my own misery had never presented itself to me before.

That week, I saved up my bus money and on Friday I went to buy two packets of paracetamol at the chemist. But they would only let me buy one. So I went to all the shops in the area and bought as many packets as I could, one by one. I got home and sat on my bedroom floor with a glass of water and started swallowing them. I must have taken 25 pills until I physically couldn't swallow any more. My throat was raw and my body was willing me to stop. I decided to lie down and have a nap.

When I awoke there was a new sickness in my chest and battery acid lining in my throat. I panicked, I didn't actually want to die, I just wanted everything to stop. The flashbacks to loud and scary fights, the bullying and molesting that I'd been experiencing at school, everything. I didn't want to feel ashamed, scared and disgusting, I didn't want to feel sad. No more hitting, no more touching.

I went downstairs and found my mum scrubbing pans in the kitchen. When I told her what I'd done, the yellow rubber gloves she had on fell to the floor. By the time we arrived at the A&E I was doubled over in pain and sweating rivers. I was forced to drink a thick black drink. Then they put a tube down my throat and began to pump my stomach.

I lay there detached as the action swirled above me in a carousel of images. Empty.

3

I was 12. Some of the local kids were already drinking at weekends and although I hated the taste of alcohol, I soon realised being drunk made everything feel better. My new friends and I started chipping our pocket money together to buy little quart bottles of brightly coloured cheap liquor. If there were too many of us, we would get a two-litre bottle of White Lightning cider. We would sit on park benches or in church graveyards, drink it all and then throw up in bushes and snog. Most significantly, the secret I learned was the power of alcohol – when I drank, I would feel euphoric, like I belonged.

Another school year ended and a new young family moved into our street, which brought some excitement to the neighbourhood. The family would talk to the teenagers on the green and let people come over to smoke cigarettes and drink alcohol in their garden. The mum was in her mid-20s, her partner was 19. Their house was sparse, but they had all the things we didn't, like a big TV, a stereo and frozen oven food. The mum spotted me smoking on the green on my own one day and asked if I wanted to come in. She let me have one of her cigarettes. She introduced me to the dad, who had a dead look behind his eyes as he watched me puff away in their empty house.

Three weeks later there was a police car parked outside their house. All the teenagers gathered on the green – the adults were twitching at their curtains or pretending to take out their rubbish so they could get a proper look at what was going on. The whole street witnessed the police officers leading the dad out the front door in handcuffs, placing their hands on his head and pushing it down into the back of their car. The rumour was that a 15-year-old girl who was babysitting their kids had told her mum that they had offered for her to stay over, and when they came back later in the night, the dad had sneaked into the spare room and abused her. The dad came back from the police station that evening and all the kids from the estate went over there for drinks. It was unanimously decided that the girl who'd accused him was a liar and was trying to get attention. The teenagers on the estate started hounding her, saying that she was a 'dog'. Only my mum said she believed her. The girl eventually dropped the charges for an easier life, but this just made our neighbours even more vindicated.

4

I was 13 when drugs came onto the scene and that's when everything changed.

Everyone I knew started smoking weed. I didn't get it, it just made me feel dizzy and sick. The weed dealer would cycle over and hand out his orders.

In June, with us all standing around him, he pulled out a baggy full of white tablets from his back pocket. We stared at the bag in wonder. The white tablets were a tenner each; none of us had that kind of money on them. My friend and I asked if we could borrow money from someone, but the dealer said we could have one on 'tick' if we promised to pay him back the following week. We vowed to him that we'd walk to school every day to save up our bus money and pay him back.

My friend chugged his half down with a beer and I copied him. We sat in silence, waiting. Then, the punch in the chest. I needed to breathe, in, in, in. My heart felt like it was going to explode. I'd never felt such a neat and potent rush of love, energy and freedom than in that moment. Life was all of a sudden full of colour and feeling. My blood felt like it was a bullet triggered in my veins, shooting through my hard, fast-beating heart.

It was on.

I didn't want the night to ever end.

Suddenly it was 4am – my curfew was 8pm. I tried to sneak in but my mum and new stepdad – a tall, dark-eyed Irishman she had met in the pub round the corner – were sitting up with two police officers. The police officers clocked how high I was straight away. They were unimpressed, but my mum didn't have a clue. She was pregnant again; and she didn't understand.

After that night, I quite quickly progressed to acid and spent my time with older, more hard-core dealers.

One night around 11pm, as I headed back across the field to our house, high as usual, I saw an ambulance parked outside. My stepdad was being led out of the house by a pair of paramedics. My mum was sitting on our wet concrete doorstep sobbing, with my granny's arm clamped around her shoulders. I'd never seen Nan being caring towards my mum in the whole time since she'd moved back to Watford a few years ago.

Over the coming days I started to piece things together through what I could overhear on phone calls to my stepdad's family and the hospitals. He had been diagnosed with schizophrenia as a teenager. He hadn't told my mum, nor had his family.

The night of the ambulance he'd been forcibly sectioned. My mum had come home from work to find her new baby Jasmine in her bouncer chair in an exploded nappy. She had no idea how long she'd been sitting in her own excrement. When she confronted our stepdad in the kitchen he had lost control. She managed to call the police, who called an ambulance.

I spent less time in the house after that.

The minute I came up from drugs, all my troubles disappeared. It was easier, better.

5

A new group of adults started to hang out on our estate. The minute I laid eyes on them I knew I wanted to be part of their gang. I was a teenage girl full of hormones, and here was a group of guys wearing tight vests, all clearly on steroids, with muscles and ponytails, who drove around in a battered van. The oldest two were in their late 20s and early 30s and had only just been released from prison. Every weekend this new group burgled and performed smash-and-grabs in the local area. They had a seemingly endless supply of drink, drugs and money. They wore heavy jewellery, had nice trainers and would turn up with beers for us all to have. We went wild with them.

I began to get in later and later and my nights became my days. I also started to fall asleep in class. One day I woke up in a classroom to my headmistress shaking me awake long after the class had finished. She told me to stay where I was.

She carried on marking work, while I sat there sinking into a pit of murky shame as the sound of the ticking clock echoed around the room. After a while, there was a faint knock, and I could make out my mum's tiny frame through the glass. She sat down and listened to the teacher tell her how worried she was about me, my mum all the while twisting a tissue in her hands, making her knuckles red with exertion.

My mum then blurted out how out of control I had become. She was begging for help. The headmistress asked me to tell her who 'those' people were that I had been hanging out with. My mum cried. The headmistress looked at her with empathy. I felt such overwhelming shame. Why couldn't I stop hurting her? Then a voice came into my psyche, *No, it's because of you. It's because of all of you,* and my shame turned to rage. Burning anger. All my self-hatred reflected onto them. I wanted to get away from both of them, anyone or anything that made me feel I couldn't escape who I was. I had an epiphany.

'I'm dropping out!'

We drove home in silence. Mum pulled up outside the house and turned to look at me. I had managed to avoid her eyes for a long time, but there they were – hanging on to me. A wordless plea. I hated the way she made me feel like shit. I knew I was hurting her, it hurt that I was hurting her, but I couldn't seem to stop myself from doing it. I wanted her as far away from me as possible, I wanted to stop feeling so lost and scared all the time. I wanted everyone to leave me alone and let me just do what I wanted. I wanted to escape my mind, not have to listen to it.

She looked back at her hands, still clinging to the steering wheel as if she wanted to take me far away from the place we had arrived at. I remained silent and she got out of the car and slammed the door shut behind her. As I watched her disappear down the path, I noticed that she seemed smaller and more fragile than I'd ever seen her before. I left it a few minutes before going in myself so as to avoid any more confrontation. The house was silent, apart from the TV that my nan kept on throughout the day while drinking her Blue Nuns. I was 14 years old.

The next morning, when everyone else was in school, I wandered into town and asked the hairdresser's where I worked on Saturdays if I could pick up any more shifts. In my fantasy world I'd just go straight to work and bypass school, crashing and smashing into the adulthood. Because of my age the manager could only give me two extra days of work, but she said she would look into getting me on some kind of apprenticeship programme, so I could at least be studying towards something. The extra days gave me just enough money to chip in and feel like I wasn't always poncing other people's drugs all the time.

A few weeks later, I noticed my older friends had adopted a new friend of their own, a broad-shouldered, classically handsome man named Danny. As soon as I was drunk enough, I stumbled over to him. I sat on his knee. He passed me a tin of beer and offered me a cigarette. After that I was his 'girl'.

He wanted sex from the start. The thought terrified me. I felt disconnected from my body. One of the 15-year-old girls who hung out with my new friends was pregnant, all the young girls they hung out with were doing it. I knew I had to do it with him if I wanted to be his girlfriend.

A few weeks into me being Danny's 'girl', the new young family on our street asked if I wanted to babysit at their house while they went to a party. They said I could help myself to cigarettes and beer in the fridge. I watched TV while the kids slept, and drank a beer. When they got back they were smashed. The mum went straight to bed and said I should stay over as it was late. The dad sat down next to me. He said I could sleep in the middle child's room as she was asleep in their bed.

I felt if I said no, he might think I believed the ostracised girl who had made up lies about him assaulting her. I went upstairs to bed and a short while later I heard his bedroom door close. I let my eyes close and started to drift off to sleep. I awoke to the sound of the bedroom door handle turning. I could feel his presence in the room. I knew then that the girl who had told her mother what this man had done to her was telling the truth.

Just as when I had been kicked in the head by the bully of a boy at school, I decided to lie still, too scared to say anything, too fearful to shout out. He sat on the end of the bed, and gently put his hand under the side of the covers. My heart screamed. He was only in the room for a minute or so. But the damage was done, the walls of my mind collapsed.

The next morning I left early and went home. My mum just assumed I'd been out all night like normal and asked if I wanted any food. I tried to eat but the cornflakes were shards of glass. I decided to have a drink instead.

You see, I had brought it on myself. I hated myself for it. I hated myself so badly.

6

I went out to try to find Danny and walked for an hour to his house. There was a sofa and broken bikes in his front garden. When I knocked his mum popped her head suspiciously through the crack of opened door. She said he was out, then slammed the door shut.

Around 5pm, I found him at The Moon Under Water pub where they all usually drank through the afternoons. I drank pints with them until it was dark and then we drank vodka straight out of the bottle, every gulp washing away this new reality in my heart and chest. Danny asked if I wanted to help them get some power tools to sell. He put his arm around me and pulled me in tight.

'Fuck, yes.'

I was one of them, I'd do whatever he wanted me to.

The rest of the night is a blur, it all happens out of pace from reality. The van rocking, speeding down the road. The doors opening and everyone jumping out. We're in a large Woolworths. The alarm sounds, and it's loud. I panic, but everyone else heads off to grab what we've come for. I look around and grab the nearest things to me – stationery. I empty the shelves into bin bags and chuck them into the van. One after another they run out, dumping their goods before going back for more. Everyone jumps back into the van and it starts to reverse. Police cars appear out of nowhere and surround us.

Danny turns to me and shouts. More police sirens approach. I decide to run. From the corner of my eye, I can see my friends being wrestled to the ground. One of the boys chucks me the police car's keys and yells at me to throw them. I see a drain by the side of the road and just as I reach it and drop them down, I'm grabbed by my arm and yanked to the ground, spun over and handcuffed. Bundled into a van, I hear Danny's voice.

'Don't tell them your real name and age . . . say you're 16, they can't contact your parents.'

We are led through the police station reception, buzzed through the door to the back and down concrete stairs. I can hear noises coming from down there. At the desk I'm asked my name, age, address. I practise my new identity. Next I am led into another room by a female police officer where I have my fingerprints taken, and my photo. Then I am asked to strip, while my clothes are checked, then put in a cell.

Just as I start to really feel sorry for myself, I hear the sound of my boyfriend yelling.

'Pigs, *cunts*, fuck your mum.'

I hear another cell door banging shut. Then it all kicks off. They are kicking against the doors, shouting at the top of their voices. The rest of the gang are put in their cells and the quietness that awaited me disappears into a cacophony of dirty football songs and name-calling. I join in and get myself so worked up, kicking and yelling, screaming 'I love yous' to Danny, that I take a run at the door, my face smashing against it, and then everything goes black as I hit the floor.

7

I study my tiny cell inch by inch. Swear words and names somehow scratched into the walls.

'GORDIE woz ere 95'

'CUNT'

'LAURIE' with a heart scratched around it.

A knock on my cell door makes me jump. The eyehole opens and I am told to answer some questions. Then the opening shuts. This is the first of my hourly check-ups.

The hours stretch by as my thoughts fill with paranoia: are the police on their way to visit my mum? What if I slipped up and gave my real name by accident? What if my friends blame everything on me? I can see my mum crumpled on the floor, broken into pieces. I don't know that 14-year-olds can't get sent to prison.

I rub my sore wrists, red from where I had struggled in my handcuffs. I hit peak comedown. I don't want to be here. New voices of others echo and I realise just how many people are locked in these cells. Only six of them are my friends. I want to be home. I have a safe warm bed at home. Every time I close my eyes I think of the neighbour sneaking into the room where I was meant to be asleep and I have to get up and pace the room to divert my thoughts.

Finally the door unlocks and the cell door opens. I've got one phone call.

I am led back through the underground maze of holding cells, wondering who is in which one. We get back to the desk, it feels like a lifetime ago that I was there being logged in. I call the hairdresser's and I tell her I've been up all night sick, my eyes catching the police officer's. He smirks. I tell her I won't be in today. She tells me she will let the boss know, and hopes I feel better. I hang up the phone. The officer leads me back to my cell in silence. I ask when I can go, but they don't answer. The door is locked behind me again and I wander back over to the bed.

Another hour passes, then the sound of the key in the door gets me standing. I am brought to the desk and given a date to return to the court upstairs. I'm not really paying attention to what they are saying – I'm out of here. They give me my stuff back in a clear, sealed plastic bag and lead me back up the stairs to the reception area. Danny is sitting there waiting for me. He gives me a long kiss, holds me tight in a hug and tells me he's proud of my silence. It's the longest I've been held in a very long time.

We wait outside, sitting on the wall across from the police station, smoking cigarettes. Then one by one our friends come out the station door. We all take the long walk back together, passing the Woolworths where we were arrested last night. The smashed windows are now boarded up. We go and sit in the same dirty old pub. People chain-smoking at the bar, the velvet seat smelling of spilt beer and the jukebox blaring out Oasis hits on repeat.

The guys get the beers in. I hate the taste of beer. But I

drink it because I like the feeling of being drunk. In fact, I down the whole pint.

Months pass as I get swept up into this cycle of endless nights and mornings waking up in police cells. I learn how to break into cars, how to hot-wire them to get the engines started. As the smallest I get sent through open windows to let my friends in to burgle houses. We get caught by the police joyriding, breaking and entering. Each arrest my name and details change just ever so slightly, close enough so I won't forget them, different enough so they don't twig I have a lot of outstanding warrants for my arrest for failing to turn up at the station at later dates, or for court.

8

Early 1997.

Time goes slowly when you're bored. When you realise you are too young to get a full-time job. Waiting for your friends to finish school, for the phone to ring. I sit on my bed and draw pictures of my hands. I stare out of the window. And I lose hours daydreaming about who I am going to be.

I learn to tell the time by the sounds of my house, my mum's daily routine: breakfast, school run, the babies' routines, dinner time, TV . . . bed.

I am regretting my decision to leave school, but I have set fire to everything. I can't turn back.

Danny and I see each other most nights. He takes me on drives down country lanes, at full speed. He buys me Reebok trainers – I've never had branded trainers before. He seduces me with all the right words, telling me I'm not like the other girls – oh so grown up. Then his hand will wander down my pants. I don't like it, I just want him to tell me he loves me and drive around so fast I become dizzy and disorientated. I also want to take drugs and get high every day.

But he wants more and is getting short-tempered. After three consecutive excuses of being on my period, he figures out I am scared. I want so badly to be grown up, but this part of adulting does not fit at all.

Danny's friends call me 'the frigid baby'. All I want is to be like them. I decide it is time.

After I've made the decision I call his mum. He is at work. I ask her to pass on a message. She seems indifferent. I ask if he can come pick me up when he finishes work.

Phone down, no going back. I go back to bed and just lie there for hours trying to picture it. I can hear my mum getting the little ones ready to go out, then her coming up the stairs. She knocks on my door and pokes her head in, asking if I will be back tonight. I don't know what to say, something has changed in our dynamic, she is no longer telling me what to do or how I should behave. She looks worn out, exhausted. I realise I have finally broken her, her fight is gone. I don't like it.

My brother senses something is up, he's unusually quiet and keeps looking at me, trying to get my attention, but I pretend I can't see him. We all eat our microwave meals in silence until the phone rings, making us jump. I run to the phone before anyone else can get there. Danny tells me he is coming to get me and to meet him at the garages round the corner in 15 minutes. I run to the bathroom, put on my newly pinched, bright, hot-pink lipstick and brush my hair. I look at my reflection, I wish I had boobs, I try to push the little I have up into my Wonderbra – a newly shoplifted item. I yell bye to the family, grab my coat and slip out the front door. Danny has borrowed someone's car and is waiting by the garage, away from anyone who would question what a grown man was doing with a young schoolgirl.

We drive out of Watford in silence. I rest my cheek against the cold, rain-flecked window, watching the town disappear and the roads turning into muddied fields. We pull up into a car park of a woodland I don't know. He takes the key out of the ignition and turns in his seat to check there was no one following us.

The car smells of old leather and petrol. I watch the birds dashing in and out of the trees, collecting food for their newly hatched chicks. I look past him through the window and wonder if I could make a run for it and hide in the woods. As my mind wanders outside, my body remains locked in the car.

'Come on, you know you want it,' he says.

All I can think of is the face of the golden boy who'd molest me at school while one of the girls pinned me against the wall.

'Come on, don't be a tease, I don't want to have to get it elsewhere,' he says, filling the silence.

Stop being a baby, Lorna.

I pull off my shorts and knickers and sit there motionless. I want to cuddle up and watch movies with my mum. I want to be back at school. I want to run away.

I've changed my mind.

Pain. Burning pain.

He moves me in the way that pleases him. And I look out of the window at the birds until he's done.

He moves me back into the passenger seat, starts the car up, zips his trousers back up, then we drive back home in silence. I try to think of something to say. I want that excitement I felt when it was wild, and we were at the police station, and he was telling me he loved me.

Nothing.

He stops the car at the bottom of my road and tells me he'll see me on the weekend, then leans across me to open the passenger door. As soon as I step out he pulls the door shut and drives away. He leaves me standing on the pavement, sore and alone.

I walk heavily back to the house, sneaking round the back door and upstairs to my bedroom. I can hear the sound of my kid sisters playing in their room next door. I don't feel like an adult, but I certainly don't feel like a child. I stare at the ceiling until my mum knocks. I want to scream. I want to shout. But instead I just say I'm tired.

He doesn't call on the weekend.

9

A week later I finally get the call from Danny. He's been busy. Out of town. He'll pick me up at six. I stand at the usual spot, going almost blind with longing to see him again, needing him in a desperate way and equally needing some potent drug in my system. I want to get high, I want to remove myself from the equation.

A rusty red van pulls up, and he winds the window down with a grin. I go over and kiss him, he winks. It's all all right. I hear giggling in the back. He tells me to hop in, he has some friends he wants me to meet. I pull open the back doors and inside are some of the usual suspects, including Robert, a kid I've known since primary school who's always up for a laugh. There are also three unknown girls who all look about my age. One of them smiles and hands me a tin of beer from a full bag by her feet. Danny hands out Es, each of us dropping half, washed down with beer.

We drive out of town to target a few small petrol stations. I've never been so far out of Watford before. The girls keep looking at each other and giggling. I notice they have big boobs. They know how to do make-up, with their flicky black eyeliner and blusher. I can even smell their hair products.

I get more and more jealous as the van speeds along.

Unable to join in any conversation, I just watch the way everyone else is pawing over the new girls. The road becomes ever more bumpy before we skid to a stop on the side of the road. Danny tells me he needs me to help him.

I get out of the back of the transit van to see an old, small, wooden two-pump petrol station. I follow Danny round to the back of it, and I notice he's carrying a crowbar. I wonder how dangerous he is. What he might have used it for before.

He has an entirely different energy, pumped and hyped up beyond recognition.

'What are you doing?' he mutters. 'Come on, stop daydreaming and give us a hand.'

I catch up with him and he helps me to climb up through the window. He tells me to grab all the cigarettes. I pull myself through the small window, but the drop on the other side is much higher than I imagined and my knees buckle. A pain shoots from my ankle, a pain like nothing I've felt before – I scream and roll around, I can't keep it together. On top of my screams a piercing alarm rings out. I look up through the window for help. Danny throws a roll of bin bags down at me and instructs me to get the cigarettes from behind the till. I say I think I've broken my ankle, he tells me to 'hurry the fuck up'.

I hate the way he's talking to me and start to cry as I limp to the till and empty the cartons containing the cigarettes into the bag, my heart pounding. I can't breathe. I am scared, but also high. I limp back to the open window and try to pass the bag back through to Danny, but it won't fit.

'Fucking idiot . . . Empty the bag into smaller bags, hurry.'

I get more clumsy the quicker I try to move. I hear Danny running the bags back to the van and I try to clamber back out of the window. The police must be coming at any moment. I look around for something to stand on to help me through the window – I find a shop stool. I drag it over, but as I am about to climb on it Danny's head pops up, asking where the rest of the packets are. I hand him as many as I can and only then does he pull me out of the window. He climbs in the back of the van with me this time. We can hear the police sirens heading towards the shop, getting louder as we set off in the opposite direction.

Eventually, we pull into a small car park in the woods, the same one that Danny took me to before. The engine switches off, the doors up front slam and we hear the sound of footsteps coming round the van. The doors open and a torch shines in. The new girls whoop with excitement. Danny jumps out first and hands out a packet of cigarettes to everyone, before giving me a hug and telling me that I did all right.

When he holds me tight, it feels so good. The smell of cheap, market-bought cologne on his neck . . . His stubble . . . I feel safe. A cassette tape is played from the van – cans of beer are passed around, and we dance and smoke our cigarettes. Danny's ponytailed friend brings out a big bottle of vodka, which also gets handed around.

My vision starts to blur and my legs feel unsteady, I try to keep dancing but I can't shake off the feeling that Danny's much more interested in the new girls. His friend offers to take me for 'a walk', but as soon as we are out of sight he puts his arms round me and tries to stick his tongue down my throat as if I'm fair game, something to be passed around. Angry, embarrassed, rage rises up in me and I aggressively push him away. I'm so confused. 'Fuck off, I'm Danny's girlfriend,' I slur at him. He just laughs and tries to kiss me again. I push him even harder this time and he falls on his ass. Now he looks pissed off and I know I have gone a bit too far. But he just shakes his head and puts his hands up in a drunken defeat, walking off and leaving me alone.

My cheeks are burning; how dare he, his laugh feels mocking, like he doesn't take me seriously. I stumble back to the party and see Danny laughing with the girls. Cheeks burning, my blood shoots round my body, heart pumping . . . Jealousy, rage. I want to pull their hair out, I want them to go away, I want it to be back to how it was the night of the arrest, just me with the boys, and all of Danny's attention on me.

I down more vodka, it warms my insides, it burns my throat and it makes me feel confident. I am his, fuck them all. I get up and dance to the drum and bass. I laugh with Robert. I try to show off. *Notice me, notice me, notice me Danny.* Like a flick of a switch it all starts to turn, the woods start moving, the world is a blur, the faces doubled, I can't focus, the green leaves above me are spinning. I stop dancing, but the world keeps moving . . .

I stumble to the bushes and fall to my knees as my insides turn out. I can't stop, it heaves out of me, pulling from the pit of my stomach. I feel like I'm going to die. I want it to stop – surely there is nothing more to come up?

Smelling the mud and leaves beneath me, I lie on the floor retching, begging for it to end.

In the calmer moments between the retching and the groaning, I find myself fantasising that Danny will notice that I'm gone and come find me, pick me up and hold me tight until I feel better, but he doesn't. Why doesn't he come find me? I try calling out his name. I lie there for what feels like hours, listening to the sound of music and laughter in the background of my bodily hell. Eventually the sickness passes, and I pull myself back to my feet and stumble back to the group.

When we run out of booze, we head back. The van bumps and skids, throwing us about in the back as it snakes along the country roads. I try to rest my head on his shoulder, wanting to feel close, wanting him to put his arm round my shoulder and make me feel safe. Make me feel loved. But I sense he is embarrassed by me. I catch her staring at him, smiling, the one with the biggest tits of all. And he's looking right back at her. Something tightens in my chest.

I look at him.

'What's wrong?' I ask.

My heart's racing and I'm panicking. He looks around to make sure he has his audience. I'm confused. Then looks me dead in the eyes and pours his beer over my head.

Silence. Robert pipes up, nervously from across the van.

'Don't be a dick, Danny. Leave her alone.'

Danny rolls his eyes in Robert's direction.

'Fuck off, you pleb,' before turning back to me. 'We're over, you're a fucking mess – look at the state of you.'

My stomach drops to the floor, and I want to meet it there. Cold, wet, humiliated. The girls don't back me up. No one does but Robert. I don't know what to say or do . . . I realise I am nothing, nothing.

I want to cry, oh God, do I want to cry, but I hold it in. As soon as the van pulls away from the bottom of my street I collapse into sobs. I can't understand why anyone would do that, I started the night thinking I had found someone that was in love with me and wanted to look after me, and here I am, early morning, on my own, walking home broken by him and ravaged with hatred for myself.

10

Another night, a month later, I lie awake for a while still wired from drugs, but now also full of guilt and shame. This is the worst part about speed and Es, the lying in bed, willing sleep to come. The morning light breaks through the cracks in my curtain. I finally pass out into a deep heavy sleep around midday and sleep right through the day and night, waking the following morning.

Alan, my new stepdad, has had another breakdown. He is now back at Watford psychiatric hospital. By the time I get downstairs, I find that Mum is already in the kitchen, scrubbing away at clean pans. The memory of Alan floats through the mist of my comedown. I go over to hug her and she stops scrubbing and her body begins to shake. She is in deep, deep pain.

'Happy birthday, Lorna,' she manages to say.

My birthday. I'd been so looking forward to this for weeks, and I had completely forgotten. Fifteen.

'Do you want your card now, or later?

'Later, why don't we rent a movie tonight and all hang out after I finish work?' I say in an attempt to clear up the mess around all of us. She smiles and I feel good again, I've done something right.

At work the staff sing happy birthday to me and on my

lunch break one of the female hairdressers, who I have a crush on, gives me a pixie crop. The staff tell me that I look like a model, and the boss even calls a photographer friend of theirs that lives round the corner to see if he can come over and take some pictures of me.

My boss asks if I would be able to open up the shop the next day and get the salon ready before the staff arrive – the assistant manager is away on holiday and she needs some extra help. I feel like I am for once being taken seriously. I want to scream and jump up and down and hug her.

It is the first time anyone has entrusted me with any kind of responsibility, and I am going to do her proud. Scenes play out in my head of how I am going to make everyone's section neat and tidy, I am going to make a pot of coffee for everyone before they arrive . . . I am going to do such a good job they will want me to open up every morning. She shows me how to work the shutters and we lock up together before leaving in opposite directions. I tuck the keys safely in my pocket, loving the sound of them jangling as I walk.

I walk to the high street to meet my mum, as she wants to take me to Blockbuster to rent a film for my birthday night.

Mum has made a curry, she's spent ages slaving away to make tonight special for me, and afterwards we have one of her birthday specials – a heart-shaped birthday cake. It is the first time in a long time we've all sat together and talked and laughed. Even though it is awful what's happening to Alan, we are together.

*

Mum is putting the little ones to bed and me and my brother get the popcorn ready. I feel warm, and happy. Then I feel it, the house phone vibrating as it starts to ring. I know it is Danny. He is ringing because he wants me back. Each ring feels amplified. I want him to see me with my new haircut. No, I'll leave it, I want to enjoy tonight, and Mum's made such an effort. Louder and louder it seems to ring. Just as I'm about to give in and answer, it stops. I take a breath. Kicking myself for not picking it up.

My mum enters the room out of breath – she's run down the stairs in the hope it was Alan.

'Who was it?'

'I don't know, it rang off.'

My brother looks at me. He knows. Then it starts to ring again.

I jump up to get it before my mum gets there.

'Hello?'

I wait. I hear breathing.

'Lorna . . .'

It's Danny. He sounds drunk. He says he wants to see me, he's missed me. He wants to explain that he hasn't been himself recently, it's the court case coming up, he is scared of being sent away again and he acted out of line. He begs me to come and see him. He wants to make it all right. He'll be at the pub.

I want to scream and roll around on the floor. He wants me back. He wants me. I keep my cool. I say I'll be there in an hour and hang up. Heart beating. Tight chest.

Then I notice my brother and mum staring at me.

I tell them it was a friend, she's just been dumped and is so upset that she needs a shoulder to cry on . . . Can Mum drop me off in North Watford?

She looks so deflated. Why can't I just stay in? Why can't I do the right thing?

'We could do the movie night tomorrow instead,' I continue.

Her eyes tell me that she knows I'm lying. Silence. Shame. Bright red burning cheeks.

My brother tries his hardest to get me to stay in; he tries guilt, passive aggression and hard stares from over Mum's shoulder, but none of it's working. I am possessed, I need to see him, nothing could make me stay in.

The drive is unbearable. Mum is deathly quiet. When we arrive I give her the biggest hug. Her tiny frame is that of a delicate glass swan. I know I should be spending my evening with them, not Danny. I let go and promise I'll come back later that night. I can feel her watching me as I walk away.

Oasis's 'Wonderwall' is playing as always from the jukebox as I enter the pub. Mostly white, racist, male football hooligans' eyes burrow into me.

Danny and his mates are sitting at a table across the room drinking bottled Budweisers and smoking from a communal packet of Marlboro Lights in the middle of the table. As I approach, his two ponytailed, steroid-induced-muscle buddies look away and avoid eye contact, as if I am an annoyance. They look like they have been here all day.

Before I even sit down, Danny asks if I have any money.

He then asks if I will give it another go. I jump onto his lap and throw my arms around him, as if it was a marriage proposal. Yes . . . yes!

I pick up Danny's bottle of beer and down it with quick, full gulps. The others stop talking and stare. Attention fully attuned to me. Danny gives me a 'what the fuck?' look, so I dramatically slam the bottle back down on the table and say, 'Happy birthday, Lorna!' Blank faces. Danny breaks first as he realises and pulls me in for a hug. Mood changes, a lightness enters the gloomy cloud hovering above them, they all hold their beers up to toast . . . But still don't offer to buy me one.

Danny shows me his hoard – acid and pills that they are going to sell tonight, so tomorrow he'll take me out to get me a present.

Others arrive and join us. Robert slides into the seat on the other side of me. When he finds out it's my birthday, he buys us both a beer and we reminisce about the last arrest while the men discuss their increasingly outlandish schemes.

A friend of my brother's walks over; he looks me square in the eye and asks me what I am up to. The way he is looking around the table I can see he isn't impressed with who I am hanging out with. He tells me I should ask to go back to school.

'It's not too late, Lorna.'

Somewhere inside of me screams, *yes, please.* Yes, I wish I was still in school right now. Yes, I want to be back at home with my family watching our Blockbuster rental. But I can't break face, I have made a decision.

As evening turns to night, and not aware of the big, full moon, we all bundle into the back of Mr Ponytail's transit van, drunk, boisterous and looking for some chaos to entertain us wild beasts. While the van bumps down country roads we all drop the acid the guys had intended to sell, then we drive around to various locations to drink the cheap giant bottles of White Lightning cider and dance in the car park next to the woods to homemade mix-tapes of rave music playing from the van stereo.

Danny on acid is something I've never seen before. His mind is exploding with the very nature of being and things – this tracksuit-wearing troublemaker, relaxed and in touch with nature for what is probably the first time in his life, is stroking trees and lying on the muddy floor, feeling the earth and bark beneath him. I feel at one with him. With this newfound love of life he gives away the rest of his drugs and everyone drops half an E on top of the acid.

Faces in the trees start smirking, the leaves rustle, I want to dance. A boy called Will is having a really bad trip; like savages or wild children we chase him round the forest and torment him.

Then blank.

Someone kicks against a metal door. It's a cell door. I know this room.

A memory comes to me, opening the shutters to the hairdresser's for them. Oh no. I shake my head, no, no, no. Drinking in the shop. Fights breaking out, the girls nicking my colleagues' hairdressing scissors and shampoo from the shop area, hell breaking loose.

11

The police. My screams as I thrash at a police officer. My fingerprints being taken, a body search, a mug shot. I wonder what the time is, I wonder if I can get out before anyone arrives at the shop this morning and I can try and fix it. I bang on the door. Danny shouts out. I shout back, saying I'm fine. Then I hear Robert, he sounds scared.

It is real this time and things are different. I've been arrested for robbing the hairdresser's I work at and I also had a fake ID in my wallet that I used for buying booze . . . That had my real address on. So, the police will finally have figured out my actual name.

I am allowed one visit that day and it's my mum. I am led to a tiny room with a glass partition separating two chairs. My mum is a shadow of herself, her eyes etched in dark circles from being up all night with my baby sister. She tells me that the police came over, they knew I was only 15, but worked out that my real record stretched back to when I was 14 and had managed to connect my fingerprints to a whole load of crimes.

She tells me that she has been warned that I might be looking at time in a young offender institution. She tells me that she has spoken to my boss at the hairdresser's, who is really upset but mostly worried for me. Although I am scared and full of shame, I laugh at her.

I am possessed. I want her to leave: if I am horrible she will go and I will stop hurting her.

The next morning we are led up to court. Our crimes are read out and Robert and I are told we will be given another date to be sentenced as we are still minors.

Back at the police station they give me my possessions and print out the agreed date for my return. My mum picks me up. As she pulls the car away I go to turn on the radio, but she whacks my hand away. She pulls the car over and screams with frustration – *Don't I care? That I could go to prison? Throwing my whole life away for nothing. FUCK!*

When we get back my stepfather is at the house again. I'm so angry, why does she keep taking him back? In shock I run to my room and cry and scream into my pillow. I wish I could turn back time. I wish my stepdad would just disappear and I wish so hard that my mum would be OK.

The next day, Robert calls and asks if I can meet him at the park, he is calling from the payphone by my local shops. Part of the conditions for my bail is that I have to stay in after 7pm. I sneak out the back door and jog down the road to meet him. Danny is with him and they both have full backpacks.

Robert tells me his dad hit the roof and gave him a beating. Danny says he has to skip town, as he will be sent back to prison this time, he is out of chances. He recounts horror stories of young offender institutions to me, how he was beaten and raped when he was our age and how once you go into that system your future is fucked – he's never met a person that managed to turn their life around once they had been inside. Robert says he has an aunt who lives in Camden who'll take us in if we need to lie low. It makes total sense to me: someone is offering me a means of disappearing, running away and not hurting anyone any more.

I go back into my house through the back door, pack my old schoolbag with clothes. I empty my kid sisters' money jar and check the kitchen cupboards on the way out – Mum hasn't done her weekly shop yet, so there's only a packet of digestive biscuits. I take them. I hear my mum upstairs bathing my sisters, I stop for a moment on the threshold of my home, what am I doing? I want to stay here, I want to be part of this family, but there is an invisible line I have crossed. I take one last breath and quietly close the door behind me.

12

Danny is silent, and doesn't reply when I speak to him. I try to kiss him – he pulls away.

The train pulls away at Camden Station and we're left standing on its platform. I've never been to London without my parents before – the sun's shining, music is blaring out from speakers on the street. Market traders, musicians playing, a sea of people pushing, walking, sat outside shops drinking booze wrapped in brown paper bags. The music slowly recedes as we walk away from the High Street and weave down some smaller streets until we find ourselves standing at the bottom of a high-rise housing estate. The tall concrete buildings shooting out of the ground appear to go up to the clouds. Robert tugs at the door and it reluctantly opens – it's been busted for years, Robert tells us as he walks in.

The block of flats smells of disinfectant, and the echoes of people talking drift down the winding stairs. We wait for the lift. When it arrives, the doors open to reveal two men huddled together smoking a small glass pipe. Their large, startled eyes lock in on us. They look soulless, empty almost, as they exhale a strange-smelling, thick, white smoke and push past us and out the heavy doors, escaping their concrete prison.

I look up at Danny. My heart aches, I need him, I need his reassurance. For the first time he smiles back at me.

'Sorry, I've been so stressed. Just don't want to go back to prison.' He turns to Robert: 'She'll be all right with the three of us?'

Robert nods. 'She's cool – she's helped me out when my dad kicked me out before.'

Danny's shoulders droop as he leans against the side of the lift. Silence. All of us watch the numbers creep up until it groans to a stop, and the doors open. Robert leads us down an open pathway lined with a security net. It's for the pigeons, apparently. Most of the front doors have metal cages covering them and some of them look like they've been kicked in several times before.

We arrive at a white, dented plastic door. Robert takes a deep breath, looks at us, back at the door, then knocks.

Nothing.

He knocks again. And then we hear the sound of a child screeching, and running footsteps. The letterbox opens and a kid's wide brown eyes and chubby fingers reach through to us. We all straighten up as a shadow approaches the mottled glass of the door. It opens a couple of inches and a wild-looking woman peers defensively out. On seeing Robert she rolls her eyes and opens the door wider, revealing a tall, strong and slightly unhinged-looking woman wearing a big, oversized T-shirt with stains down its front.

The kid is about two, he's only wearing a T-shirt and looks like he needs a good bath.

'What'd you do now?'

I focus back on the aunt. Robert looks at us, then down at the floor, trying to work out what to say.

'We got in some trouble, can we come in?'

She tuts as if she was expecting him to turn up at some point, and steps to one side, motioning with a nod of her head for us to come in. The flat's dark, all the lights are off, she must have just woken from a nap. The further into the hallway we go, the mustier it feels, the whole place smells of piss and smoke.

We follow Robert to the living room while his aunt shuffles off to fetch us some water. The curtains are closed. We all sit on the saggy sofa and the kid bounds in and starts to climb all over Robert, which breaks the awkwardness of this unknowing.

The aunt comes back in with glasses of water, then falls into a stained armchair and roots around the side of the seat before pulling out a blue packet of Rothmans cigarettes. I watch in awe, she is so defiant looking, stern almost, her hair looks like it hasn't been brushed in weeks. I watch her as she takes out a cigarette and places it between her teeth, lighting it, then takes a long, slow inhale. Her head tilts back as she looks down her nose at us while she slowly exhales.

'I got a call from your dad looking for you, he's majorly pissed. So what happened?'

Robert rehashes the version we had planned while on the train from Watford. We didn't realise they were going to burgle the store. We just asked for a lift home, and the court said we'd be sent to prison. Danny pipes up, looking the aunt dead in the eye. Gesturing towards us, he says, 'And you know what would happen to *them* in a YO, right?'

She gives him a nod – they seem to have a shared knowledge of this world, whereas me and Robert know nothing. Whatever he says works: she takes another pull of her cigarette, then tells us we can stay for a short while, but we'll have to get work and help out, look after the kid and stuff. Earn our keep. And not, under any circumstances, tell anyone where we are staying; she could lose her kid if social services find out she is harbouring us.

Our bodies relax and Danny looks at me and smiles. Hope. It is going to be all right. She asks if we have any money on us. Silence.

'Any of you got anything?'

Robert shakes his head. She pulls herself up from the armchair, walks over to the window and takes a tin off the ledge, pulling out a baggy of yellowy white powder. I know what it is. Nothing tastes worse than speed, even looking at it makes me retch. But I understand her now, she's a speed freak. She raises her eyebrows and offers it around.

The kid runs feral around the house and sits right up to the TV, watching kids' programmes for the rest of the day while we smoke, speed is snorted and rave music played from her hi-fi's tape player.

I feel awkward: it's wrong, I'd never do this around my kid sisters. Lost in a time bubble I catch sight of the kitchen clock and realise it is now nearly 9pm, and the kid hasn't eaten. I ask the aunt if she wants me to make him dinner. She just swats me away, telling me to look in the cupboards.

I feed the kid tin mush, but he is more into the buttered bread I've put on the side. He starts yawning, so I run him a small bath, clean him up and he falls asleep while I carry him to the aunt's bedroom to find some PJs for him.

I sit at the end of her bed. Her room stinks of stale air and unwashed sheets. It is full of boxes, and piles of stuff. Like a hoarder's lock-up. I lie him down and hunt around for some clothes, find some nappies, and end up putting him in one of her T-shirts, tying the bottom to make it into a onesie

Back in the living room the aunt has slipped into the sofa next to Danny and Robert. The night continues until the sun starts to rise. The aunt brings some blankets for us and Robert goes to sleep on the armchair. Me and Danny spoon on the sofa, but I am too wired to sleep. He starts dry humping me and tries to get my knickers off. Normally I would be too insecure to say no, but right now I don't want to do anything sexual, with Robert trying to sleep across from us, in this unknown flat in this unknown city.

13

A little bell rings as I push open the door.

I was taking the kid out for a walk when I spotted the sign in the window of the small, family-run hairdressers – 'Help wanted'. I wait at the reception and tell the kid I'll buy him some sweets if he behaves and I look around. Nanas under hood dryers, men sat waiting for the barber to get to them. The smell of relaxer and coconut shampoo. After a while a beautiful soft woman in her 50s comes over and I ask her if they are still looking for help. She looks quizzingly at me and asks if I've ever worked on Afro hair? I lie. Yes. She looks to the kid.

'I'm babysitting for my friend.'

She nods again.

'Yes, I know this boy.'

I can't suss it out.

She tells me that I would be washing hair and assisting the hairdressers. Ten quid a day and she'll train me up. She asks when I can start. Right away. She tells me to be there at quarter to nine tomorrow morning. I take a card with their phone number on just in case. I thank her and leave to the tinkling of the door bell.

I want to do cartwheels down the road. I want to throw

my shoes into the air. Filled with excitement, I skip with the kid along the arches back towards the concrete tower.

I have too much energy in me to go back to the flat just yet, so stop at a little run-down park nearby to let the kid play. I chase him around the park and follow him up the climbing frame and try to teach him how to play tag. He doesn't quite get it, but he screams with laughter when I chase him pretending to be a crocodile. Then we carry on back to the flat.

Both Danny and Aunt are sleeping. Passed out cold. When she finally gets up she stomps around the house, not thanking me for looking after the kid. Robert tells me not to worry – she's always like this on a comedown.

I tell them about my new job which lifts the mood a bit, but they take the piss out of how much I'll be getting paid. I don't care. Aunt wants us to get her some cigarettes and food. Danny only has a fiver left, so we plan to buy the cigarettes and shoplift the rest. We get dressed and head out as a trio to explore, promising to come back with everything she needs. We go to the job centre and look at the jobs advertised on the pin board.

'Fuck it, may as well sign on while we're looking.'

Not taking into consideration that we are wanted by the police, Danny fills out dole forms, then Robert takes us for a tour of the area. We pick up cigarettes and have enough money left over for a beer, which we share between us in a park. With the sun shining, Camden feels alive. The few sips of beer seem to change the mood for everyone and things start feeling like an adventure again as we talk about the future and making plans – to get jobs, go on holidays and to get our own flat to share. It feels like the beginning of the rest of my life, and the whole world is there for our taking.

Our shoplifting expedition turns out pretty lame, and we end up being followed around by weary shopkeepers, only managing to lift Tampax and toothbrushes, so we decide to call it a day and head back. We tell Aunt that Danny will be getting his cheque in a week and I will be earning money from tomorrow; she seems proud of us. The next morning, she accosts me as I try to leave without waking anyone. She reminds me to ask for payment at the end of the day.

'Just tell them you're broke and need an advance.'

I grab my coat and leave, full of anticipation, nerves and excitement. I hear her voice shout out to me as I close the door.

'And see if they can sub you tomorrow's too.'

I take a moment to breathe. I have got so used to the smoke in the flat that it is only when I go outside and feel the fresh air, I realise how grim it is inside.

I stop outside the shop and peer in through the glass front. An old-school hair salon. A community hub. Elderly women sitting under hood dryers having their hair set. The boss, an older lady, relaxing someone's hair, her husband cleaning up a teenage boy's hair with clippers. I want to make sure I am so good that they will never not want to have me around. I push open the door and the little metal bell rings. The husband's forgotten I am starting. His wife comes over and greets me with a smile.

She sets me to work straight away, refilling bottles, sweeping, cleaning and washing hair. I make sure everything

I do, I do really, really well. At the end of the day she says goodbye and thanks me for doing such a good job. She'll see me tomorrow. But I hover. Too embarrassed to ask, but too scared to go back to the flat with nothing. I swell up with embarrassment but deflate back to size when she offers me the money.

I walk back with the burning happy tenner in my back pocket.

The smoke hits me as soon as I open the front door, but this time I can smell they've been smoking weed. I can hear the kid screaming with laughter, Robert is playing with him.

Aunt doesn't look at me, just puts her hand out. I hand over the money. Danny is lost in a computer game and doesn't even acknowledge me, so I go over and sit beside him. Nothing. I drape my body across his for a cuddle, but he keeps playing, his joint hanging from his mouth as he mumbles to himself.

I stroke his face.

'I love you,' I say.

He looks down for a beat and then carries on playing.

My instincts are ringing, something's happened. Something's off. I can feel Aunt's gaze burning into the back of me. What the fuck is going on? I get paranoid, did the police come looking for me? Are they going to ask me to leave?

Chest burning with anxiety and awkwardness, I have to speak up, I finally push the words out from my stomach.

'What's wrong?'

Aunt tells me that my mum has got hold of her number

and has called looking for me today. She had turned up at Robert's house banging and screaming. The police will be coming next, so I'll have to look for somewhere else to stay. Blindsided, I ask what is going to happen to Robert and Danny. Robert says he's probably going to go home tomorrow as his dad will have calmed down by now. Danny just shrugs.

I have nowhere to go, and even if I wanted to, I feel like I can never go home now. I think of my brother. The police. My mum and what I am putting her through. I have done too much to go back.

I can't talk or I'll cry, I need to breathe, so I go to the bathroom and lock the door behind me. Then it comes, crashing and pouring and burning. I fall to the floor – tears, burning eyes, sickness from the bottom of my stomach. I can't breathe. I'll beg Danny, I'll show him we need to stick together, that we can find somewhere, I'll get another job. I'll find a way. Desperate, heart palpitations, hyperventilating.

There's a quiet knock on the door. I try to compose myself, slow down my breathing. Splash my face with water, patting it dry as I look at my reflection. Dark circles. Red eyes. It finally calms.

I hold the door handle and unlock; I take another, slow, deep, breath, then open the door to find Robert standing there looking like he's been crying too. He says we should go back and deal with it together. His eyes. They are scared, and contain pools of sadness. He too has witnessed pain as a child, he too is searching to find people or places to fit in. His fear a mirror for my own. But I don't want to be that,

I want to be fearless, brave, I want to show everyone that I'm an adult.

I accuse him of abandoning me. I say I am going to get another job tomorrow and find somewhere to live. He begs me to change my mind. No way, I tell him, no, there's no way I'm going back. He shrinks, almost disappearing, and leaves me in the bathroom to cry some more, until there's nothing left.

Danny is rigid when I sit back down next to him. I try to run my fingers through his hair, but he pulls away as if I have an infectious disease. I fall asleep wrapped in a blanket and wake in the middle of the night alone. I know he's in Aunt's room. I am desperate. I'll forgive him. I've been too clingy. I can change. My mum calling has scared him off. I'll make him see that we could have a life together, that it's me he wants.

At the end of the next day's work at the hairdresser's, I collect my daily wages and run all the way back, I need to see Danny. We need to talk. The door is on the latch when I get to it. I open it, I can hear the TV blaring and the whole place smells of weed. As I take off my coat I hear a grunt. I edge closer to the kitchen, the noise grows, I know what's happening but I could still be wrong. I push open the door and I find Danny doing Aunt from behind against the kitchen surface. My eyes are on fire. My soul is punched right out of me and I fall backwards to the floor.

The pain. The shock renders me still, mouth open, a knife cut right through my core, my very being a vibration of energy so extreme I don't know what to do. Then I remember to breathe and everything comes crashing back to me, my soul, my energy. The adrenaline.

I throw my bag at them and run straight at Aunt, I want to rip out her heart, I want to scratch her skin, I want to punch her and hurt her like my heart is hurting. Danny pulls up his trousers as I jump onto her, lashing about like a wild animal, but she grabs my hair back and slams my head against the kitchen surface. I call them names, I scream and scream. I see Robert's face appear at the door, his face drops in shock and he runs to help me.

'Get her the fuck out of here by the time I get back,' Aunt shouts to Robert.

She storms out of the kitchen, pulls on Danny's arm and they leave the flat with the kid, slamming the door behind them. Robert won't look me in the eye. He knew. He knew.

But still I can't go back to Watford. What the fuck am I to do? It's not an option. Impossible. Robert has had enough and tells me he is leaving, that I should go home with him, I can stay at his place if I need to. I shake my head. We look through the *Yellow Pages* and ring a couple of numbers for hostels – he knows all about them, as his older brother has left home and is living in one. Most of the ones we speak to are for over-18s, only a few would take over-16s. We finally get through to one that has space on Brewer Street in Soho. The guy explains that it is a 10-minute walk from Leicester Square, and Robert scribbles down the directions.

We walk along the chaotic busy Camden streets to the tube station. The first time we walked these streets I was an embodiment of love, overspilling with adventure. But now we both feel heavy, legs made of solid lead. I catch sight of Danny in the park with Aunt and the kid, he can see me, I know it, but he looks away. My heart breaks. Robert links arms with me and pulls me along. We jump the tube barriers, Robert holds the sensors after someone passes through and I go closely behind him. The escalators lead us deep underground to get the Northern Line straight to Leicester Square. The tube rocks and sways, the carriages are full. Me and Robert have nothing to say.

I am a shot animal left to bleed out.

14

Soho, London. Spring.

I step into the hostel's waiting room. If I sprint out the door I could probably catch up with Robert. But no, there's no going back.

I close my eyes and pray. Please take me in. Please help me. Please.

The receptionist watches me with what I think is concern. I notice he's wearing brown corduroys. I look at his face. Yes, he's safe.

Past his left ear lobe is a hang-out area. I spot bodies and laughing mouths. I want to see their faces. I want to meet them. I look back at the receptionist, he's still waiting with his eyebrows raised. He repeats, 'Can I help?' His auburn hair has a kink in it, so I focus on that to help the lie seem less self-conscious.

'My mum kicked me out, and I don't have anywhere to stay. I'm 16 . . . Nearly 17. My brother said you had space and that I can stay here?'

He is a normal, kind person, not a whiff of drama or danger about him. I feel safe for the first time in what feels like a long time. He asks my name and date of birth.

'Tammy.'

He asks for my surname. 'Dayden.' He digs around a little more and I can tell by the way he watches me that he knows I'm not who I say I am, and that I'm not 16. I wait as he scribbles something onto a form.

He pushes paperwork through the plastic screen's gap and asks me to fill out my details and sign at the bottom. I sit on a plastic chair in front of him and fill in the form, giving an old friend's address and adding my new date of birth. I look at the posters pinned up on the wall – Childline, Samaritans, Citizens Advice and other helplines. A missing poster of a teenage boy, 16, 'High risk due to his age'.

The receptionist tells me they have a bed for me, I'll be sharing with another girl. But I have to get him my National Insurance details as soon as possible.

I hear a voice, a whisper, 'And tell me who this little girl really is.' I look at him, but his mouth isn't moving.

I follow him through the canteen and dining area, I can pick out Irish, Scottish, northern accents, all young, all wearing tracksuits, girls with permed hair, boys either with short-cropped gelled hair or wearing baseball caps. They are huddled together, sat on chairs, tables, eating chips. They stop talking and I can feel their stares as I pass.

I follow the receptionist's shadow, memorising the footprint of this new building, one corridor after another and up two flights of stairs. He makes small talk and then stops and gives me a kind smile when he knocks gently on a metal door.

'Yeah?' a girl's voice replies quietly from the other side.

He opens the door to the room and I edge in behind him. It's a small but bright room with two bunk beds either side, and lockable side cabinets. On the bottom of one of the bunks is a young Somali girl reading a Bible. Her hands are rested on her extended pregnant belly. She looks too small for her swollen, bursting stomach. She carries on reading. I drop my bag and look around the room.

Silence ripples.

The receptionist asks if I'm hungry.

I look down nervously at my feet, not saying anything. He seems to understand and tells me to come to the kitchen.

'They serve the best chips around. I'll shout you a plate.'

He drops me off back at the dining room and tells the woman serving that he'll give her the money later. The canteen lady gives me a wink as she shovels a large greasy portion of chips onto a plate for me

'There you go, sweetheart.'

I sit at an empty table one up from the group and eat slowly, hoping they will notice me and invite me over. I listen to what they are saying, it's gossip about one of the other girls staying there. I watch them out of the corner of my eye as I eat the chips as slowly as I can. I watch the way they talk and move – laughing, cocky, slouched back in the plastic chairs. I like the way they dress, the boys mainly in Adidas tracksuits and baseball caps, the girls low-slung jeans and tight vests. I can't make out their ages, but it must be varying from 16 to 21. I want to introduce myself . . . I have to. If I don't I'm on my own. And I know I can't survive on my own right now.

One of the boys catches me watching – I quickly stare at my chips and feel my cheeks burn. I can see his figure nudging his mate, I can feel the table's eyes on me. I hear the chairs screech as they are pushed back and feel the shadow of the guy and his friend coming over to me. For a second I panic, are they going to attack me? No aggression, just smiles. They introduce themselves in thick Scouse accents, then ask where I'm from. Do I know anyone else around here? I shake my head. They ask if I want to come hang out at the park with them and their mates, motioning towards the others at the tables. I look in their direction. I'm in.

It's a deep, in-my-very-nervous-system type of relief. Everyone introduces themselves, it is a bold, brash mix from across this tiny island – two boys from Newcastle, a boy from Liverpool, two girls from Manchester and another from Glasgow. There are only a few other 'Londoners', teenagers from the suburbs, all kicked out, from low-income families, all kicking back with a fuck-you attitude.

With no real plans or even an idea of what is going to be my next step, I finish up my chips, my stomach finally full. We pick up tickets from the reception which turn out to be luncheon vouchers that can be redeemed for a meal and drink from McDonald's, local cafés and other fast-food restaurants and we head out into the sunshine. Feeling the sun on my face, the uneasy, scared feeling from only a little earlier dissipates, and with each step, each in-joke I'm taken into, this new beginning feels more and more exciting. A fresh start with people who don't know my real name. My past disappears, I am new.

This is my first introduction to the constant flow of homeless people that always have and always will come to London in search of a better life. Most of the kids are escaping poverty, abuse, violence and, like me, the police.

We arrive at the big black metal gates to St Anne's Park, where we meet up with a bigger group of people. I've never seen anyone like the people hanging out here before. As I sit and watch wide-eyed, the old boys come and tell me stories from when they were in the army – their smell is almost too much to handle. My new friends notice my unease and tell me not to worry – it's as if they can't smell what I can. I can't stop staring at everyone, taking it all in.

Some are already drunk and others seem to be high, but comedown high, eyes drooping, still awake from the night before. Some are young teenagers staying in hostels. Some are young street homeless, some are old boys who have been here more years than they haven't; bad teeth, browned nicotine-stained fingers, hands clutching cans of Tennent's Super.

A few men are in combat fatigues with large backpacks by their feet, there's a Canadian couple who have matching dreadlocks and hemp trousers. There are also a few young girls who you can tell aren't homeless. One is a tall pretty blonde, she's wearing a nice outfit, everything matches and I'm jealous. I wonder why she's here. She's deep in conversation with a beautiful younger homeless guy, a mop of brown curly hair, laid back, wearing a leather coat over his vest. It's too hot for leather coats, so it must be his look.

It is around 3pm when parents and nannies start to walk past the park with kids in school uniforms. I think of the little boy I'd been playing with just that morning. I wonder what kind of future he will have.

The curly-haired guy cracks open a beer from a plastic bag by his feet, hands one to the blonde girl, his pirate friend and then offers one to me. He throws it before I've answered, we crack them open. I've never drunk so early before. Some of the kids I'd come with leave, some others arrive. As we sip our beers I watch and absorb the scene, a young teenage mum with bleach-blonde hair and a tiny baby in her arms turns up, she is showing everyone a freshly inked tattoo on her arm of the word 'Snacker' – in memory, I am told, of the baby's daddy, a homeless man that died of a heroin overdose only months ago.

I listen to the old boys tell me more drunken stories of their army days, stories of bravery and saving their comrades, surviving bomb blasts, only to be forgotten once they returned. One of them is so drunk he pisses himself while he sits talking to me. As the day goes on we all drunkenly help with the baby. I stay out with my new friends until just before nine, when I realise the others from the hostel have already left, and only the two teenage boys from Newcastle are still there. They round me up, drunk and incapable of walking straight, and herd me back.

A different receptionist buzzes us in and scolds us for being late, he tells us this is our first warning, we only get three before we are kicked out. Like naughty schoolchildren we try not to giggle as he buzzes us through to the main building and we separate to the different sides of the hostel – boys and girls. I try to be quiet as I sneak down the hallway. I can hear people talking in hushed tones from behind the doors. I unlock the door to my room and tiptoe to my bed so as not to wake the pregnant girl. The blinds are open and the street lights outside give a soft glow to the room, I can see light shining in the whites of her eyes. She is still awake and has been crying. I ask if she is OK, she doesn't answer, just pulls her covers up and turns to face the wall.

Her sadness fills the room.

15

By the time I wake the next morning the pregnant girl has already left. I go down to the canteen, where the Newcastle boys are sitting eating breakfast with their bags packed on the floor by their feet. They say they are leaving because they find London 'too hard'. They haven't been able to find any work and don't want to end up on the streets like the others. They have decided to go back home and try their luck there. They give me a hug and tell me to look out for myself and be careful, then finish their food and leave. I sit in silence, feeling sick and empty again. The receptionist passes through and asks how I am settling in. I smile. He asks me to hand over my National Insurance number today. He really needs it to submit the forms, I can use the phone to call around if I need to. I can't think straight. The reality of what I am doing is starting to sink into the marrow of my bones. I say I'll try.

I collect my luncheon vouchers from reception and head out into Soho alone. Walking down Berwick Street, I stop to stare through the sex-shop windows on Walker's Court. I continue walking and notice an advert for 'dancers' above a doorway on Rupert Street. I descend the low-lit stairs into a reception area smothered in red velvet. Cosseted within the walls, an overly made-up woman greets me. I tell her

I need work and could start right away. Without saying a word she disappears through a string-bead doorway, then returns a short while later with a tanned overweight man who invites me into the back, explaining the rules of the 'club' as we go. The first room through the beads is small with mirrors on the walls. He is out of breath even though we have only walked a few steps.

'Full nude dance is twenty, no touching. If he wants more you call in the house mum.'

We carry on walking through to another back room which has a dinner table, chairs, a small kitchen and a fridge.

'Cash up front, always,' he says earnestly before asking me to pull down my panties.

I blush. I can't think of anything more embarrassing. He's waiting. After a few wheezy breaths he nods down towards my crotch.

I nervously unzip my jeans, then pull them down. He rolls his eyes and nods for me to remove my knickers too. *I don't want to, I don't want to, I don't want to.*

I take a deep breath. He glances at my crotch. I know I am a late developer but it doesn't seem to bother him. He smirks.

'Come back at one and bring something sexy. You should dress up as a schoolgirl, the customers will love it.'

He nods for me to pull my clothes back up. Nothing more. He didn't ask me my name or age.

I go out to look for my schoolgirl outfit.

I duck into a sex shop and head straight towards the back section to check out the porn mags. I have never seen one before, just heard of them from my brother's friends, there was one boy on the estate that had one they would all look at that he kept hidden under his pillow. But I need to research what 'sexy 'looks like. None of the girls in the magazine look like me, they are all big-chested, tiny-waisted with long hair and golden tans, they even have nice-looking tanned butt holes. I am pale, tall, gangly, with short-cropped hair.

From there I head to Oxford Street to scout out the security in the shops. After a couple of close calls I manage to shoplift some thongs, which I've never worn before, a pleated miniskirt, a shirt and some knee-high socks from Topshop, then I head back to the club. As I get closer to the doorway I get scared. *Actually, what the hell am I doing? I've changed my mind, there's no way I can do this . . .* But another voice tells me I need the money.

So, I dress up in my new outfit. It isn't lost on me that most of my friends from school will be wearing their actual school uniforms in my old classroom right now. I don't have any shoes, only trainers, so I decide to go shoeless and just walk around in my knee-high socks. When I am dressed, I report to the house mum behind the desk and she tells me to go and dance in the doorway and call out to men on their own. My job is to lure them in for a dance with me. I'm not sure what to do, but notice there is another 'dancer's' doorway across from me, so I copy her every move.

Within five minutes a man approaches and asks how much for a dance. I am too nervous to reply, so I motion for him to follow me and lead him downstairs. Arriving at the bottom I point to the 'house mum' sitting behind the desk.

She explains the rules to him in a cold, flat, leaden tone before extracting £20 off him for a striptease.

He sits down and as the music begins and I try my best to dance, yet my legs shake uncontrollably. I wiggle around and every now and then I remember to take off some of my clothing and fondle my adolescent boobs. As soon as I awkwardly remove my knickers, the guy grabs me and tries to kiss me. His sweaty, shaky hands are now all over my body, grabbing and slobbering at my skin. All I can see is the sweat above his top lip as he pulls me towards him. I scream and try to push him off. The security guy comes in and drags him off me, charges him extra for breaking the rules, then chucks him out. The security guy then comes into the room and tells me off for dancing too close.

'These men can't control themselves, you have to be smart,' he says brusquely in his deep Russian accent. 'Be more careful next time.'

I go back upstairs to dance in the window. I spot a group of kids from the hostel passing by and they lock eyes with me – they first do a double take, then crack up into fits. The bouncer comes back up to see what all the commotion is about and they run off. Dread and shame clutch at my chest. That afternoon, I have two more customers, both as bad as the first, then I finish my shift and leave for the evening with 30 quid in my pocket.

The pregnant girl's stuff is gone from our bedroom, she must have been moved on. I lie down, desperate for a rest, I feel weightless, falling, until a knock at the door makes me jump. The receptionist introduces me to my two new roommates, Tracy and Kerry, a wild pair of girls from

Manchester – Madchester as they call it – both curvy and short with permed bleach-blonde hair and both wearing twinset Adidas tracksuits. They ask my name, where I am from, how long I've been here. They are full of questions, buzzing to be in London, and dying to get out and about. They tell me they have run away to London in the hope of getting scouted to model. I sleep deeply and soundly. I dream that my teeth keep crumbling and falling out, I try to talk, but they just fall into grains, I spit them out crying, all my teeth gone.

The sound of whispering voices pulls me out of my dream. It takes me a moment to remember where I am and that the two girls from Manchester are in the room with me. I watch them.

I suggest we should hang out in the park with my friends, but as we pull up to the park gates and they see the type of 'friends' I have they roar with laughter.

'No way – we're not going to hang out with those smelly tramps.'

We decide to go to Goodge Street, to a pizza place that takes the luncheon vouchers, and we fill ourselves up on bread and soda. The vouchers give us a centre point to the day where we can sit and eat like normal people. In the early evening we drop our stuff back off at the hostel and I raid my savings from yesterday before heading out with the girls to buy a half-bottle of vodka and some cigarettes from the local off-licence. We swig straight from the bottle and walk around Soho as they look for young, rich tourists who, they say, will take them out dancing and buy them drinks. We don't meet anyone to take them out, but we get steaming drunk. They begin to throw glass bottles at walls and pick fights with other girls. They are loud, brash and confrontational. I join in, we are like wild animals, kicking things, screaming, laughing. As we yell at the night, anger I've held deep down finds a new outlet and the more rage I throw out into the world, the more free I feel. Let it out, Lorna, let it out, the voice in my head whispers, and I do.

Kerry, the taller of the two, tells me to wait by the metal railings outside King's Cross Station and walks across the road, stationing herself on the corner of the street outside a McDonald's. She approaches travellers hovering around outside the station with ease and before long she has 'scored a win' with a stocky, tall fella. She leads him down an alleyway across the road. I begin to learn how to differentiate 'us' from 'them'. I watch commuters running into the station with purpose, and drunks, dealers, prostitutes and homeless beggars waiting for the trade to come out of the station. Kerry comes out the alley 15 minutes later with two £20 notes and is swigging vodka to 'remove the taste of his cum'. It is only then I understand.

We buy more booze with her money and wander the streets causing even more mayhem; the girls slur abuse at tourists and then we try to smash shop windows and kick over bins with a wild, unfiltered rage. Their anger becomes more and more personal and they attack a lone woman for no reason.

We arrive back at the hostel around midnight and the night receptionist buzzes us into the reception area, but refuses to let us into the actual building because we are clearly intoxicated. He says we can wait in reception until morning if we want, as we need to sober up. He reminds us of the vulnerable people upstairs – it would be dangerous for the others if he let us in.

Kerry kicks off, swearing and shouting, smashing against the front door with her fists. He says he'll have to call the police if we don't stop. Then Tracy whips her pants down and pisses on the reception floor. The receptionist picks up the phone and we all scrabble to open the locked door, shit, it won't open. Kerry kicks her foot at the door, breaking the pane of glass. She bends down, removes the sharp spears of glass and pulls herself out. Tracy and I drop to our knees and quickly follow her, bursting out onto the streets, howling into the moonlight.

After the adrenaline wears off the reality of our situation hits us: we are cold, drunk and have nowhere to go. We try to talk our way into a couple of nightclubs but none of the bouncers are letting us in. We decide to wait it out, huddling under our coats in a doorway, trying to doze until the morning. A few times I drift off briefly, but each time I wake my hangover feels worse and a heavy, overwhelming headache is pulsing harder and heavier until at around 5am Kerry gets up and declares she's had enough and that they should go home to Manchester. She helps Tracy get up. The trains will be running again now, she says, and Tracy agrees they will come back when they have some money and somewhere to live. I walk with them up Tottenham Court Road to Euston Station, where they scribble down their phone numbers and addresses before they jump the barriers and blow me a kiss, disappearing into one of the carriages. And just like that they are gone too.

16

I stand there staring at the carriage door they disappeared into, hoping they will change their minds and hop back out, but after a few minutes I realise they won't, they are going home. I feel totally alone and pretty fucked. There is a Watford train waiting at another platform, as if it is waiting to take me home. I don't get on board. I need to keep running.

17

Homeless.

I curl up with my knees tucked in my jumper in the fire exit of a theatre. The walls emit the smell of years' and years' worth of piss and dirt, but I can't think where else to go. I eventually nod off, curled up in a ball on the flagstone step floor. I dream that I am in a womb, everything is deep pink and warm and I can see the light breaking through skin, I can hear a mother's heartbeat . . . I feel warm and safe, I'd like to stay here forever.

I wake up to the noise of a car horn and a child screaming from its pushchair as it's hurried past my curled-up body. Everything is pink, still, like it was in my dream, but I recognise it now as the bright sunlight piercing through my eyelids. I peel them open, and the hot, relentless sun is beating down on my sweat-riven skin. I sit myself up, dry-mouthed and hungry. I look around and try to bring back last night. I've got no clue how long I've been asleep or what time it is, but there's a leather jacket laid over me. The jacket has that musty, dirty, homeless smell to it and I look around to find its owner.

I spot a guy selling The Big Issue across the road: he is tall and thickset with big, dark, kind eyes and stubble so thick you could light a match on it. We catch each other's eye;

I smile at him and he nods back as he takes a sip from his beer can.

I notice that just past him in the park is a big group of kids. Some dozing under a nearby tree, they've clearly been up all night. Others wide awake, skinning up and drinking beer. My eyes lock back onto the *Big Issue* seller, who has just sold his last magazine and is picking up his bag and opening another tin of beer.

I follow him into the park. My stomach groaning, I have nowhere else on the planet to go. The *Big Issue* seller walks right over to me and introduces himself as Patrick. He asks if he can sit down next to me and whether I still need the coat. I hand it back and we talk a little. He says that I shouldn't be sleeping in doorways as it is too dangerous round here. I don't know what to say, he asks if I need money to get home or if there is someone he can contact for me. I tell him I can't go home, the police are looking for me and the hostel has thrown me out.

'Come on,' he says in his gruff voice. 'These guys will keep an eye out for you for now, but you want to find a girl to hang out with. I don't trust any man around here.'

He takes me over and introduces me to some of the group. The two tall guys that I had seen join last are Canadian; they are the friendliest of the group and invite me to come sit next to them, passing me a joint and introducing themselves. Ben and Liam. I ask them where they sleep and they tell me they are pitched up on Berwick Street outside the Co-op. I have never heard the word 'pitch' before, so ask what it means. They tell me everyone round here has their own pitch – if you leave it for a week anyone can take it over, unless you are an old-timer, then no one fucks with you. I learn that they have only been around for a couple of months, saving up to get flights home. Apparently they had a live-in job at a pub but got into a fight and lost their work and their place to live overnight. They don't want to stay in a hostel because hostels are dangerous. They tried it at first but kept getting their stuff nicked and say that, 'If you weren't a junkie when you went in, you'd be sure to leave as one.'

Everyone in this group goes by a street name: there is a guy called Para, who has been in Iraq and on his return home suffered a breakdown with PTSD. He is short and stocky and has tattoos all over him, but he is clean-shaven and doesn't smell. He is going out with 'the crazy Spanish girl' who has schizophrenia and is always starting fights with the other girls. She is the only one in the group who won't acknowledge me.

There is 'Skinhead', who has a Borstal tattoo on his fist and tattoos on his face. He has an air of danger about him. I learn that Borstals are juvenile prisons for boys, known for their brutality. They have all been drinking in memory of Skinhead's friend, who was due out today, but killed himself a few nights ago.

Then there is a fair-skinned Irish girl called Orla with long, jet-black hair. Her eyes are giant pools of blue with virtually no black in them. That's the heroin, they tell me. I have never met anyone on heroin before.

Then, as the sun starts to lower in the early evening, Orla's cockney boyfriend Macca turns up. He is in a mood because apparently he's had a slow day begging and had to go all the way to Marylebone to make some money. He is handsome in a gruff way, tall, stocky, but with a slouch, and there is something disconnected in his eyes, like a child trapped in a grown-up's body. He is really stoned.

Apart from him, everyone else has run away to the city to be saved and they have instead found one another. No one's stories quite add up, much like mine, but if you end up in this group you have issues and it is an unsaid rule that you don't question anyone's past.

When nightfall comes, Para lends me his sleeping bag because he has just been given a bed in a hostel in Vauxhall. Patrick pulls me aside from the others, really drunk and unable to stand straight, swaying to and fro, and asks me again if there is somewhere I can go. He says he can give me the money to get a train ticket and clumsily starts to look through his pockets for cash. I shake my head, I tell him the police are looking for me to send me to prison, and say I want to stay with them. He says I can't stay with him. He finds a note in one of his pockets, hands me a fiver to get some food, and shouts to Orla to keep an eye out for me, before drunkenly walking off to make his way to wherever it is that he goes at night.

Orla and Macca take me to Golden Square. Macca fetches some cardboard he has stashed in a bush and makes it into a makeshift mattress for us all. They tell me more about the others; I ask about the blonde girl who I had seen with the tiny baby and they tell me that her name is Karlie and that she had been going out with their friend Vaughn. He was 17 and from the care system and had real anger issues as well as being a heroin addict. They had split up early on in the pregnancy and he'd started seeing the pretty blonde girl with the nice clothes from a few days before. He had recently gone to a detox centre, but relapsed when he came out and overdosed on methadone. He had died and left Karlie alone with the baby. They are worried that the baby is going to be taken off her.

We say goodnight and get down into our sleeping bags. I drift in and out to the sounds of sirens and drunk people singing and fighting. All these noises are even more amplified in the cold spring night air with no walls to shield them.

That was the first night I properly slept on the streets. It would go on, on and off, for 14 months.

When I awake the next morning, Macca is already rolling up his sleeping bag. We hide our bags and the cardboard in the bushes of the square and then we go to The London Connection so we can shower and get clean clothes. The Connection, as everyone calls it, is a drop-in centre for the homeless, somewhere you can see a doctor, get therapy, do your laundry and even get a decent hot meal. Orla tells me to wait in line to speak to one of the helpers there and to tell him a fake background when I register with them. She also tells me to say I have an appointment at a hostel in Zone 6 so I will be given a blank travel card. After we eat she takes me to Charing Cross tube station and manages to sell the ticket for a fiver to a person queuing up at a ticket machine, then she shoplifts various items she had written down on a list. Afterwards, we sit on the top deck of the bus back into Soho and as I look down at the busy streets and the sunshine breaking through the hectic skyline I don't feel as disconnected.

We get off at Piccadilly Circus and wend our way through the back streets to the brothels near Rupert Street where we visit a few prostitutes of varying ages: some young and full of life, a few old, weathered and with a take-no-shit attitude. These aren't like the prostitutes I had seen in King's Cross. None of them are high, or seem like they are on drugs. They are safe and this is their job. They have taken on flats, some are shared, the rooms turned into bedrooms catering for different kinks. My eyes are burning – this is a world I wouldn't have imagined. There is even a 'granny' sat in one room knitting. And these are the ladies that Orla is dropping off her wares to in exchange for cash, while taking more orders for her next 'shop'. When she is done she counts through her money. She gives me a fiver for helping and we stop at the off-licence to pick up some beers on the way to the park.

When we arrive we see that Karlie, the girl with the baby, seems to have partnered up with Skinhead – he has his arm around her and they are sharing a joint while she holds the baby in her other arm. Macca is already there, swaying with a drink. I down my beer, hating the taste but wanting to get drunk. I know that I only feel relaxed when I am pissed, so I gulp it all down in less than a minute. More joints go round and more Tennent's Super cans are cracked open.

Karlie asks if I can hold her baby for her while she goes to get more drink. This tiny little being is dropped onto my lap.

It makes my heart ache. I look at its miniature fingers, its tiny, tiny fingernails. It's much smaller than either of my sisters when they were newborns. As with the little boy in Camden, I wonder what kind of future it will have. This ball of innocence in such a bizarre place mothered by a girl–woman who thinks she is broken but is still so innocent. After a while Karlie comes back with another bag full of beers, and we carry on drinking until Patrick turns up. When he sees the state of her he tells her to get home and put the baby to bed. She tells him to stop being a prick. He grabs her arm tightly and asks, 'What would Snacker think if he was still alive?'

She puts the baby back in its pushchair and leaves.

Patrick comes and sits down with me. He warns me about Orla and Macca's smack problem. He tells me that they are constantly getting themselves off the streets and trying to turn their lives around, but the drugs keep ruining them and they always, always end up back where they started. He looks deep into me and says, 'Keep clear of drugs. I've never seen anything destroy people's dreams and ambitions more.' He has the friendliest, saddest eyes I've ever seen.

18

Patrick, the *Big Issue* man was right, Orla's and Macca's addiction was taking over again. We were out shoplifting when she pulled me into the public toilet cubicle and said she wanted me to keep her company. She was talking nonsense, fixated with the ritual of preparing the needle. At first I didn't want to watch and looked away, but I could hear the change in her voice the closer she got to injecting it: her intensity, her obsession with it interested me. I turned around and saw she had a rubber tube tied round the top of her left arm, her left fist pumped with urgency.

As she slipped a needle in, my eyes drifted up her arm to the numerous bruises and pockmarks of scabs . . . Then back to her face, then back to the needle. It was hypnotic, the way the syringe pulled the blood into the liquid, a little red swirl, hovering within it, before being plunged into her system. When she was finished she pulled the needle out, blunted it on the wall and chucked it into a bin. She had changed, in that moment; it was clear she felt no pain. She was floating around in life.

Macca had started to get red, sore abscesses on his arms as his veins collapsed and became infected. Nowadays, he had to inject into his hands, leaving them scarred and swollen. The same dotted scars adorned quite a few of the people I knew – some even had them on their necks. I had become able to differentiate the look of the heroin addicts from the fast-paced crackheads. Patrick and his gang were just drunks and they would either fall asleep in their own piss or disappear into the night – maybe they had a bed at a hostel, maybe their own flat. Patrick was always disappearing, sometimes for days on end. Come to think of it, everyone was. It was hard to know who was really homeless, and who had lived this lifestyle so long that even when they were housed they couldn't leave the life behind.

As Orla and Macca were now more often high than not, I started to help out with their shoplifting when she wasn't feeling well, as they needed more and more money for gear. I had come to know where all our friends were pitched out around that square mile of Soho, so when days were slow, I would pop over and visit the northern lads, or pinch cigarettes off the Canadian boys.

I drift off in the park to the sound of Orla and Macca arguing with each other in hushed voices. It has been happening a lot more lately.

The sound of a lighter being flicked meant they were beginning to prep their gear, the burned caramel smell of the smack wafted into the darkness of my sleep.

A now very high Orla shakes me awake. Wild eyed and agitated, she asks if I trust her.

'Yeah, I trust you.'

I sit up, freaking out, worrying that something has happened. She strokes my face and looks at me in a way she has never done before.

'Macca likes you. *Really* likes you.'

She leans in to kiss me. It takes me a few seconds to figure out what is happening, then I pull back. I feel sick. No, please don't do this, we're sisters, we're friends. She can see I am freaked out and shushes me.

'It's OK, you'll like it. Just relax . . .'

She leans in and kisses me again, I don't know what to do, a million things race through my head. If I say no, she may not want to spend time with me any more. She pushes me back so I am lying down and I freeze as she kisses my neck and unzips my sleeping bag. I hear Macca sitting near us, groaning. I try to focus on what he's doing, I see his shoulder jumping. She slips her hand down the front of my tracksuit bottoms and starts touching me. I just lie there motionless, if I just let her get on with it, it will be over quickly. Then another person's hands, Macca's hands, touch my small breasts and Orla pulls down my trousers. After half an hour of me corpsing they give up and start bickering and smoking more heroin. I am unable to sleep, worried – have I made things worse because I wouldn't get involved? I don't feel safe any more, my body won't relax. The day starts to break, I wait for the usual morning ritual of packing up and us all heading to The Connection. But Orla won't look me in the eyes, into the air between us she says that they have to go get themselves clean.

When they leave I let out a deep, guttural cry. I sit on the bench in the park, watching people on their way to work, couples holding hands and a mum pushing a pram. I want to go to work, I want someone to hold my hand and I really want my mum.

19

I am dreaming that I need to escape something awful when the first blow to my head comes. I open my eyes and see a girl's face twisted with anger screaming down at me. Then her fist comes at me and lands somewhere on my face. She is screaming, but I can't make out what she is saying. I try to scream out too. She kicks me in the ribs, multiple times, then her voice starts to make sense . . .

'I know you're sleeping with my boyfriend!'

The kicks to my body cause shooting pains in my sides. I pull myself into a ball and finally manage to scream for help.

'If you ever touch him or even speak to him again, I'll kill you!'

Sparky, the boyfriend, appears and finally pulls her back and puts his arm around her. I am confused. In pain. In shock.

A few hours before this attack, Sparky had raped me in a public loo. He'd lured me to a downstairs public toilet in Carnaby Street – it was 'safe', he said, for us to smoke up. I hadn't understood why we weren't going to the park to smoke a joint like usual. He'd pulled me into a grim toilet cubicle and got out a glass pipe. I'd seen something similar when I used to hang out with my stoner friends.

He'd fiddled around and put something on the end, then he'd lit it, taking a large inhale. His eyes had glazed over as he held the smoke in.

When he exhaled the thick white smoke, I'd realised it was something else. I'd never smelt anything like it before. He'd put it to my lips and nodded for me to inhale as he was lighting it. It was strong, but as soon as it went into my lungs I wanted to keep sucking, keep going, and when he'd taken it away I'd held it in for as long as I could. My heart had been lurching out of my chest and my head had felt the lightest it had in my life.

It felt incredible.

Sparky had taken another hit, then he'd pulled me close, telling me to open my mouth. He'd leaned in close, so close his lips were almost touching mine, but I wanted to get as far away from him as possible.

Blowing the smoke into my mouth, he'd tapped my arm, urging me to inhale. I did, and took it in as deeply as I could. I'd wanted the rush again. But this time, after I'd held it in for a while, just as my head had felt like it was going to explode, he'd stuck his tongue in my mouth. Without thinking I'd flinched and pushed him back, then fear had hit me as I had no idea how he was going to react. He'd looked at me with his dark eyes, wilder than normal, and it was then he'd pushed me up against the wall and put his hand over my mouth.

Full of adrenaline and my whole body throbbing, I sit up and let the tears run. I am hurting. But I am also angry, I have been severely abused by both Sparky and his girlfriend in the space of a morning. I limp to the Canadians, Ben and Liam, and shake them awake. I know my face is in a bad state when I see their shock.

'Jesus fucking Christ! Let's get you sorted out.'

Ben goes to find me some painkillers and stuff to clean me up. I have two gashes on the top of my head that are bleeding and the skin under my eye has split open. Liam asks what happened and when I tell him he kicks the lamp post, I've never seen him like this. No one has ever been angry on my behalf before. He paces up and down talking about what he is going to do when he sees Sparky. An overwhelming pain shoots through my head and makes me cry out. He lies me down and strokes my hair, then tells me that I can't be everyone's friend out here.

'Never trust the men out here, even the good ones. It's survival, and even the best ones, on drugs, are capable of the worst.'

Is he talking about himself? I don't know what to think anymore.

I look at the amber-coloured squiggles on the foil, he has another little rolled-up tube and hands it to me, telling me to suck up the smoke and chase it along the foil. I do what he says and hold it in; as I exhale, a lightness comes over me and I am extended into a space outside of guilt and pain. A warm glow bathes over me. I ask for another, there isn't much left but he lets me have the last of it, until no more fumes rise from the liquid. Then I curl up in Ben's sleeping bag and float off into a world where everything is all right.

Liam interrupts my dream world to sit me up, but I don't

mind. I let him clean up my wounds and try to glue my skin back together with Super Glue, keeping my eyes closed so I can stay in this floating world. He shakes my shoulders.

'Are you OK? Open your eyes, Tammy . . .'

I open my eyes and smile at him.

Everything is finally OK.

20

I know he is a police officer straight away.

He walks over and crouches down.

He tells me he hasn't seen me around before.

I feign ignorance, he flashes me his police badge. I tell myself, just be calm, Lorna, they don't know who you are, make up a name; do not give it all away.

I watch his every move, and he doesn't take his eyes off me either. He opens his rucksack and takes out a radio handset, a pen and notebook. He asks my name and date of birth. My heart racing, I feel like crying, running and hitting him all at once. I look past him down the street and wonder if I could outrun him. I could go through Chinatown, get lost in the crowds maybe, or down one of the side streets where the towers of rubbish live. But then he would be looking for me. I try to slow my breathing and not let him see how terrified I am. I give him my fake name and date of birth. Inside, I am consumed by a hungry fear. He calmly calls in my details. He tries to make small talk as we wait for his radio to crackle back with identification of my existence.

'Why are you here?'

'What do you want to do with your life?'

'It's dangerous out here . . .'

'People get murdered all the time on the streets . . .'

To this I respond, 'If that's true, why's it not in the newspapers?'

'Because it's not entertaining enough, no one cares about homeless people,' he replies.

The radio crackles.

No record.

He slowly puts the radio and notepad away. My read on him tells me he is contemplating taking me in, but instead he crouches down to my level and tells me to get off these streets and that there are plenty of places he can put me in touch with. I shake my head. I exhale my contagion of terror as I watch him disappear into the busy crowds.

The more I cry, the more people slow down and the more money gets dropped into my lap. At first I cry because of the shock, and the fear, then I cry because people are giving me money.

A few hours later the post-work human traffic dissipates, so I get bored and wander round to the park to see if anyone is there yet and find the beautiful curly-haired boy Seb sitting on a step sharing a beer and a big bag full of Pret sandwiches that they leave outside their stores at the end of every day with one of the older boys. I only realise I'm starving when I see the food and nearly rip the packaging off a large ploughman's baguette with my teeth. Seb laughs, waiting for me to finish, then stands up with his arms outstretched to greet me with a big hug. He smells clean and he has a similar aftershave to my dad's. I want to keep hugging him because I think I love him, but I also want to keep hugging him because being wrapped up in his warm arms and him smelling the way he does reminds me of a safety I had forgotten about.

More people arrive and the group expands, along with more multipacks of beer and a big bottle of vodka. Seb comes back into my view, skipping towards us. Jumping from foot to foot, he can't contain his excitement. He checks around to make sure no one else can see us, then pulls out a baggy from inside his coat pocket with a ton of Es in. He was going to sell to everyone here at cost and then sell around the clubs later: he can charge whatever he wants inside.

We head down to hang out at Leicester Square and wait for the others. The square is packed full of tourists and people out on the razz. Girls in tiny minidresses tottering on towering heels that they can't walk in. Men doused in aftershave and wearing their shiniest clothes. Families with kids holding balloons and the buskers out in force, playing music, beatboxing, a guy playing a traffic cone as if it was a saxophone. The epicentre of the city is chaos.

Seb walks on his hands, Ben the Canadian dances until his trousers split leaning forward, then has to stay sat down for the rest of the evening. Everything is hilarious to me, I've never had so much fun. Sparky turns up and sits right next to me. I smile at him as I don't want him to know he scares me. I lock eyes with Seb, hoping he can read my thoughts, I'm begging him to come over and help me. He puts an end to his conversation and coolly comes to sit on the other side of me, shakes hands with Sparky and asks how his girlfriend is.

'In Holloway, out soon,' Sparky replies with a smirk.

Seb tells Sparky he is in a hostel at the moment and

applying to go back to college. Sparky doesn't budge and the conversation opens up to the group.

When everyone seems to be here we walk en masse to clean ourselves up in the McDonald's toilets. All my new friends now have on their best clothes and clean faces. No one would ever know that they were homeless and living on the streets. As we get closer to the bouncers, Seb takes the lead and shakes hands with the burliest of them, then motions with his hand to us and we are ushered through. I've never seen anything like it. Sweaty men, dancing with their tops off. Dancers on podiums. Seb seems to know most of the people working in the club; he cuts the queue to the bar and comes back with shots for us all.

We come up on our Es and the night is a sweaty mash of dancing and euphoria. The boys take their tops off, so I take mine off. As a hard, fast track booms through me, I have a moment of neat, terrible panic, it feels as though my heart is exploding out of my chest.

I watch two guys' mouths in slow motion.

'Are you all right?'

I shake my head. Then over Liam's shoulder I spot Seb walking back onto the dance floor with an older guy, who slips him something that looks like rolled-up cash. They kiss and part ways.

Time falls back into place, everyone's voices are now returning to their usual frequency and the music takes over my fluctuating heartbeat. Seb asks if I want to go out and get some air. I still can't talk, so I just nod.

The sun is rising and we decide it is better to sleep under a tree so that we won't get moved. It takes ages to fall asleep, lying there as the sun rises and the park fills. It must be around midday when I finally drift off to the rumble of the busy city.

21

Spring/Summer 1997.

It was a hot, sunny day when fate introduced me to Toni. A weird smell lingered in the air, as if Soho was rotting right from its centre. Bin bags were piled up everywhere – I'd heard there was a strike – people were walking down the street holding napkins to their faces.

I was zoned out, tired. My stomach was churning with hungry, jabbing pains. I'd slept in and missed The Connection, and woken with a sunburned nose.

The Canadians had been looking after me for a few weeks – I'd bed round the corner on Shaftesbury Avenue and they would check up on me.

The memory of the smack which Liam had given me had begun to haunt my days. It had made me sick for a bit, but underneath my reaction a deep yearning had finally been fixed, albeit briefly.

So there I am, daydreaming about smack and staring at the beautiful Chinese girls above the shops across the road, watching them pour out tea in illegal gambling places, when a woman's animal cry brings my eyes back down to street level.

There are two people across the road having an argument.

I can tell they are crackheads by their crazed energy. Anyone on crack moves at fast-forward speed. The woman is pale-skinned with wild curly hair and the guy I've seen around before, he's lost half his teeth, has a ponytail and always wears a wooly hat, even on hot days like this. I can't help laughing at the two of them arguing as he throws his arms in the air and shouts at her to fuck off before storming off himself. She turns around and catches my eye, flashing black anger at me.

I nod my head up as if to say hi. She does it back, then, checking that no cars are coming, runs across the road to me. She comes right up to my doorway, blocking out the sun. It flares around her curly hair. She tells me that I have taken her spot, she has been away for a while but is back now and wants to reclaim it. I start crying, I can't help myself. I am so angry, I know I am supposed to be tough and not let people mess with me, but I can't help it.

She sits next to me and asks if I am all right. I wipe my eyes.

'Look, don't worry, it's fucking brutal out here, I should know. I've been around for four years on and off.'

She smiles reassuringly, then offers out her hand.

'Toni.'

I shake her hand.

'Tammy.'

'What happened to your face?'

I start crying again. She puts her arm around me. Between sobs I tell her about Sparky and his girlfriend.

She tells me no one will mess with me now that she's around – if they do she will kick their fucking heads in.

She says if I want she could pitch up across the road later on and keep an eye out for me for a bit. She winks at me with her big blue eyes and touches the side of my face. I smile back even though it hurts to do so.

'Toni . . . Toni . . . You coming or what?'

Her toothless friend has come back and is yelling for her from across the road. Whatever they were fighting about seems to have been forgotten, and I can tell he's just scored as he is as giddy as a child.

'I'll come see you later, stay out of trouble.'

She squeezes my shoulder, as if to say it's going to be all right now, then runs over to her friend to continue with their mission.

I continue daydreaming in my doorway, in the nothingness of empty thoughts, right in the heart of the stench of the city. The upper-floor windows above the shops are like TV screens into another world. I watch as men sit smoking cigars around tables, with beautiful women serving them drinks. It's hypnotic. I wonder who these people are, and what their lives are like. Do they have children? What do they eat for dinner when they are at home and what TV shows do they watch? Are they looking forward to a holiday with friends this summer or are they scared of flying?

My eyes drift down to the restaurant below, filled with well-dressed people and happy families laughing and eating. I think back to my home – we never ate out, we couldn't afford it. Once or twice on my mum's birthday my gran would treat us all to a Harvester buffet, and we did get a fish and chips take-out on occasion, but this family look like they are used to eating out, plates left still full of food. God, I'm hungry. I wait in my doorway, scared to go anywhere in case I miss Toni's return.

The two boys from Newcastle who had been begging at Piccadilly Circus have just packed up for the day and they come to hang out, full of cheeky swagger. They bring me sugary tea. We all sit on my step and they show me the new baseball caps and hoodies they've pinched from Lillywhites, the giant sportswear department store by the Eros.

They tell me that one of their friends from around here is now in prison and looking at doing 12 years, so they are going to have a drink for him. Why? For mugging someone with a knife when he was high.

'He wouldn't 'ave stabbed the guy, he just wanted to scare him. He's an idiot for getting caught.'

I know that everyone round here is capable of doing things when they are desperate, Patrick has warned me about that . . . But the thought of any of my friends pulling a knife on someone drops horror into my calm. When you become part of this world, the outside world moves further away and your focus becomes circular – there is just this one-mile-wide world of constant drama. That's all we talk about: who is up to what, who is in prison. What we are going to do that night . . .

After a while they go off to score some weed and I go back to my dreams.

I too have begun to blend further into the sights and smells of the city. People have started to give me a wide berth as they pass, and instead of handing me change they drop it on my sleeping bag. Sleeping in my clothes, day in and day out, while sweating in the spring heat, has given me the smell that repulsed me when I first arrived. My clothes have started to darken with dirt, taking on the colour of moss. I notice my nails are almost black and my hands are brown with dirt. I hide them under the sleeping bag. I'll have a shower at The Connection tomorrow, when Toni comes back and knows where I am.

I pick up a Coke ring lid from the pavement and begin to excavate the dirt from beneath my fingernails. Waiting for Toni, who, though I don't know it yet, will change my life forever.

22

I try to claw off whoever is trying to touch me.

I come round slowly and realise it's Toni. She has a big wide smile that splits her face in two. She puts her arms around me and hugs me tight, soothing me like a child. I notice she has a weird white crust caked on either side of her mouth.

'Come on, let's get some food, it'll help calm your nerves.'

I eat a Happy Meal quickly, hungrily, filling myself for comfort. She has ordered a Filet-O-Fish, but is just staring at it. She is right, I feel much better after the food starts to settle. We sit across from each other in silence, smiling.

'Want to get out of here and go for a walk?'

We walk out onto the street, but she is speaking and walking so fast that I can barely keep up. She shares some of her story as we walk – she's been on and off the streets since she was 15. Her parents kicked her out and she's had nothing to do with them since. The council gave her a flat once, but her neighbours had it in for her and used to tell lies to the housing people, saying she was selling drugs and working as a prostitute from the flat, and eventually they kicked her out. She got her neighbours back, though, by putting petrol through their letter box and setting it on fire.

I have that rage too, I can see how the flames could soothe the anger inside me.

We snake our way back to Soho Square, but the memories of Orla and Macca keep invading my thoughts. I scrunch my eyes shut, trying to push them out of my thoughts. Orla kissing me.

I need a drink, something to stop my mind from remembering. Drink will help. It always does.

I tell Toni I want to get something to drink.

We buy cans of beer and a quarter-bottle of vodka to swig, then settle down in the busy park and sprawl out on the grass. I watch her roll in one smooth continuous motion the perfect joint before lighting it up and taking a long inhale. All the while her eyes are fixed on me.

'See, that's better. Your shoulders have relaxed. Your whole body's changed.'

'Have you got anything else?' I ask.

She lies back on the grass and stretches out her whole body, letting it relax. She hands me the last of the joint, rolls another and continues to share snippets of her story.

'I've just got out of Holloway, was set up for something. Why you not in school?'

I tell her the truth about the young offender threat.

'You done the right thing. They don't rehabilitate kids, they fucking destroy them,' she says, taking another drag. 'I never seen one kid go through the system and do all right.'

I know then I have done the right thing, for me and my family.

'What about your parents? Is your dad still around?'

'They're dead.'

'We make our own family,' she says. 'The street family is all I have too.'

23

'Come on, I've got a treat for you,' Toni whispers.

I follow her to Rupert Street, where she approaches a guy hanging around an electricity box. They make small talk, shake hands and then he kisses her, right on the mouth. Jealousy, rage and confusion rise up inside of me. She starts jogging back to me and grabs my arm, pulling me down the road, skipping. When we're near the NCP car park she takes something from her mouth.

We go through the fire-exit door, down the concrete stairs and into the subterranean darkness. I follow her deeper underground until we hit the bottom: a dead end by another fire-exit door. I notice there are used needles and cans scattered about under our feet. It's dark and gloomy down here, but there are some piercing, scattered shards of light breaking through the railings from above. The air is saturated with disinfectant and piss. Toni clears a step at the bottom of the staircase and I sit down alongside her, eager to see what this surprise is. The ball she spat out is wrapped in clingfilm and she places it delicately on the step, then pulls an empty drink can out of her pocket, knocks a dent into its side and rests it between her knees.

She takes out one of her stud earrings, then punches five or so small holes into the dent. She then takes out a cigarette, lights it and passes it to me, instructing me to smoke it while holding it straight upwards, so the ash can't fall off the tip.

She puts her earring back in its hole, then takes the cigarette back and taps the ash over the holes in the can.

She passes it over and tells me to hold it carefully. Again I do as I am told. She quickly retrieves the small clingfilm ball and carefully unwraps it, revealing an off-white/yellowish little rock. I recognise what it is straight away, it's the same thing I smoked with Sparky. In that moment on the stairs, I understand. Her wired nature, the hungry look in her eyes.

She begins to prepare it using her thumbnail to break off a tiny bit of the rock and gently place it over the ash that rests over the holes she has made, then quickly rewraps the rock and puts it in the small coin pocket of her jeans. She takes out a lighter and puts her lips around the drinking hole of the can, holding the lighter's flame to the rock. Then she sucks in the smoke as far as her lungs can expand. When she reaches capacity she removes the can from her lips and gulps some air to push the smoke down deeper into her lungs. Her eyes fall shut as she passes the can to me.

She motions for me to suck through the hole. Her body has collapsed into itself, a high-pitched groan escapes her voice box as she eventually exhales.

If Toni is doing it, I want to do it.

So I inhale deeply, filling my lungs with the thick white smoke, then the air to bring it deep into my bloodstream.

BOOM

BOOM

BOOM
BOOM

My heart's pounding takes up all the available noise. Somewhere far away I am aware that Toni is already smoking more.

But my mind is screaming with euphoria.

Fuck the world.

Fuck everyone back in Watford.

Fuck the police.

Fuck anyone who used to matter.

I have everything I need right here.

I want more.

I reach for the can again as she prepares more.

'Calm down, I'm sorting it!' She smiles. 'I knew you'd like it.'

I can't hold it in any longer. 'I'm so glad we found each other,' I say.

'Me too, but thank fate, that's what brought us together, you don't fuck with fate . . . Just think, everything we've done in our lives, from conception to childhood, was planned to bring us together.'

She lights another rock, holds it in, pulls me close and I breathe in her second-hand smoke.

'Don't ever wish any of that bad shit didn't happen to you, as it was part of the path set to bring us together. Everything you've been through made you who you are. And you are amazing, Tammy.'

I am meant to be here, me, I, you . . . Now.

I want more, I watch her holding in the smoke, my eyes

now hungry like hers, eyeing up the can . . . She exhales and passes it over. This time I put the flame straight to the rock and smoke it until there is nothing left. Toni doesn't stop me, she just laughs, takes the can back when I am done and prepares herself some more.

I laugh at all those men who have tried to hurt me.

I feel like screaming, 'Fuck you! '

I am godlike.

All time becomes centred on the size of the rock between us.

We'll show all those fuckers, we will.

I am god.

Then the rock is gone.

We pick up our sleeping bags and, with them slung over our shoulders, go to Leicester Square to look for Liam and Ben. Seb is there too. He gets up, puts his arm round Toni's shoulder and reminds her of what happened last time.

'Don't mess with that shit, you've too much to lose.'

I want to know what he is talking about, I want to know what happened.

She slips out from under his arm.

'Stop lecturing me, I just got out of fucking prison, just celebrating is all, so give me a break.'

She motions with her head for us to leave.

'What's wrong?' I ask.

'Nothing, come.'

As soon as we're out of earshot of the others she tells me.

'Just heard my mate's been nicked, and he's got the best patch in Soho, so we gotta hurry.'

We walk down Charing Cross Road, take a left at Leicester

Square and arrive at the strip club Stringfellows. We hover around as she checks that no one else has pitched up begging there.

When she is sure the coast is clear we sit under our sleeping bags together by the cashpoint, begging the smart-looking perma-tanned men going into the club. She is right, we make a killing. At least a hundred quid in a couple of hours. She tells me to keep going and she'll get some cigarettes and drinks for us.

Twenty minutes later she is back with that now familiar cheeky look in her eyes and says that it will be quiet now until one, when the club closes, so we might as well go and have fun.

We buy one rock at a time, promising to save our money. Everything is focussed on the next rock, on getting the money to make it ours. All my thoughts. All my body.

As soon as the rock is used up, we're back out on the hunt for more. We find a dealer down the side of one of the clubs, hanging out by the bins. He looks really messed up. His jeans are hanging down, revealing his boxer shorts, and he has a long beard. He hands Toni a small, blue-wrapped ball of heroin. She asks if he has any foil. He rustles around in his backpack and pulls out some old, used scraps. He points to me.

'What happened to her?'

'Some drunk guy,' Toni says.

The guy nods, *Of course it was.*

24

We use crack every day; its endless mania, the constant cycle obliterates everything else.

I don't have time to think of what has happened in my past, my family, nothing, I become lost in a chaotic cycle of begging, finding punters, buying crack and smoking it in various NCP car parks in Soho.

We are lost in the shadows where no one can see what we are doing and how we are surviving.

When I am high everything is heightened, the outside world drops away and it is just us, and it feels like I have everything I've ever wanted. We begin by only using heroin in the mornings to level us out and help us sleep. That yellowy-brown powder feels like nothing I'd ever felt before: from that first time I smoked it I knew I needed it – it smothered me with love. The insanity of crack soon becomes something I do to get to heroin's sweet, final destination. A deep sense of being loved.

Everyone else blurs out of view.

One afternoon Toni has disappeared again while I was sleeping. My body and mind crave to cross over into the dream world, but I don't have enough money to get any gear yet, so I decide to distract myself by trying to nick an

Adidas tracksuit from Lillywhites. I walk in, holding myself tall, oblivious to my stink. In my head I am here buying something. I notice some young Japanese tourists looking at me and whispering to one another. My face burns up, I look down to my hands, seeing how dirty they are, not just my nails but the whole hand. I've forgotten to go to The Connection to have a wash, I'll go there after and sort myself out. I manage to find a pair of trousers without a tag, I wander around for a bit, then just brazenly run out the shop doors and don't stop until I make it to the car park round the back of Brewer Street.

At The Connection I find Seb in the canteen, eating chips. I keep my head down and rush through to the other side of the room, I don't want him to see me until I've had a shower and put on my new trousers.

While I'm in line, I poke my head into the laundry room, where they keep boxes of donated clothes, and ask if they have any T-shirts. The manager brings over a box and I rummage through. I find a cute white polo shirt and a pack of underwear. I have a long warm shower and wash the dirt and grime off myself, black, dirty water swirling down the plug hole. As I wash my scalp I feel some scabs on the side of my head. I switch the shower off and step out into the tiny bathroom. I part my hair and look in the mirror. Orange crusts and oozing sores criss cross all over my head. I'll come back tomorrow and see the doctor, I think. I get dressed and look at myself in the mirror, I love my new outfit and I feel good. I stuff my dirty, smelly clothes in my backpack and jump up the stairs as fast as I can.

Seb's eyes sparkle when he sees me and he gives me a big grin.

'That really suits you', he says, nodding to the polo shirt, 'it makes your eyes shine.'

I blush as I slide into the seat across from him and eat his leftovers. He asks so many questions.

'What brings you joy? What subjects do you like at school?'

'I love art, but I'm not very good at it,' I answer between bites. 'At school my biggest frustration was that I was always being told by teachers that I didn't understand because I didn't pay attention, but it's not true – I lost attention because I never understood any of it and they made me feel stupid for even asking. I don't have a clue what I could be.'

'You don't need to have it all figured out just yet . . .' he says, putting me at ease. 'Most people don't really figure it out until they're much older. Some people want nine-to-five lives, some people want to be their own boss. And artists, that's a completely different thing all together, it's a way of life, it's the way you look at the world, then translate it through your ideas . . .'

An atomic bomb goes off in my head. I have never met anyone before who's said, 'You will figure it out in your own time.'

He grabs my arm gently. 'Come with me, I want to show you something.'

We walk just round the corner from The Connection, then cross the road until we are standing outside the big wooden doors of an incredible building.

'The National Portrait Gallery.' He looks at me with

those big shiny eyes. 'There's so many places you can go for free to look at all the great artists.'

We step through the revolving doors and into the building. I am breathless even in the hallway. High ceilings, huge echoing rooms, full of art. Paintings hung on walls, people in nice clothes, big groups of schoolkids, the place full of people taking in these incredible paintings. He shows me it all: old oil paintings, modern portraits. I can't believe people can paint like this, and that Seb knows about places like this. It feels like I am suspended in time. He shows me one painting which brings me to my knees. The luminescent skin. The light so bright it almost blinds me. How can a human hand create such beauty? It feels like a bolt of lightning. The closest thing I have ever had to a religious experience.

'I like to come sit and read in here sometimes. When I first discovered it, I gave myself homework and set about learning all the names of the paintings, and then the artists.'

We leave and he points out the Charing Cross Road Library.

'When it rains you should go back and write down the names of your favorite painters, then read up about them in the library. It's my favourite thing to do when it's dead outside.

'Come on, let's see who's at the park.'

Patrick is at his pitch, selling his magazines, when we get there, already half cut and in a jolly mood. He puts his arms around me and Seb and pulls us in to his wavery hug.

'How you been? Had to sort out family stuff.' He ruffles

my hair. 'You need some food in ya, kidder, you're all skin and bones.'

I understand then that this weird, gruff drunk with the kind eyes really cares about me.

The usual crowd is inside the park larking about, and I am shocked to see how much bigger and chubbier the baby is. It disorients me; how long is it since I last saw them? I must really be losing track of time. Come to think of it, I don't even know what day it is. It makes me think of my baby sister – I wonder what she looks like now. That terrible empty feeling in my stomach opens within me and it shows me its claws. I need Toni, I need something to take away these feelings.

I am on the edge of the fun, looking around and thinking about how I can get some gear. Seb had taken my mind of it for a while, but now I can't sit still, and my thoughts are obsessing over it.

Seb says he is going to check up on Liam and Ben, so I go with him, desperate to find something to block out the feelings that had entered into me when I saw that baby. I hope the Canadians will have some gear on them.

As sure as day, we find them gouched out in their usual spot. Neither of them has any gear on them, though – they are both using methadone now, prescribed by doctors. They don't need to panic anymore where their next hit will come from – the NHS is willing to fund it. They aren't the same happy, silly men anymore. They are lost in the pull of the methadone blanket. They smell bad, too, even more than when I last saw them. In between nodding out and coming to again, they talk about getting their break soon. They'll turn it around, they say, they just need that one good person who will pay for their tickets home.

Seb sits next to them, no judgement whatsoever. He listens to them, asks them how's their day been, or fills them in on gossip. Their faces coming to life and twitching with smiles and nods as he delves into who is doing what/ sleeping with who. I notice an angry, yellow, pus-filled abscess on Ben's hand. It looks pretty bad. I try not to stare, but Seb catches my look.

'Hey, mate, anyone looked at that?'

'Nah, it's all right, It'll clear up, just got to stop using the vein.'

'You should get someone to look at it anyway. Why don't you go to the walk-in? I'll come with you?'

Two ghosts look back at him.

25

As soon as the tip of the needle broke my skin, it was as if my world became microscopic. What must have been the tiniest amount on the tip of the needle entered my blood and I could immediately taste it at the back of my throat.

Metal and medicine.

I felt warm, I wanted it, I wanted it all. I looked up and Toni looked back at me, the tease, I needed it. She looked back at my arm. She pulled the syringe up, a tiny slither of my blood danced into the clear liquid.

Then she slowly pushed the plunger down. It rushed through my veins, warming my whole body as it was released into my bloodstream. It was better than anything I had ever felt before. It was instant. It was beautiful.

26

I never wanted to smoke crack ever again, that feeling of being so up, rushing, the intense heartbeat, the missions, the chaos, I didn't want it anymore, I wanted heroin's deep, deep warmth. I fell back and back and back, into the earth, deeper and deeper, out the other side, and into space.

27

While my addiction grew, our world became smaller.

28

I had one target: to retreat. My family was a distant memory now, and almost didn't feel real, like they really were dead. I would wake up in the cells of Charing Cross Police Station and not know how I got there. Charges for shoplifting were read out in Hammersmith Court. I'd get released in the end, numerous false names and ages, being turned back out onto the streets, walking all the way back to Soho.

Sometimes I'd come home to our patch, cold, in the middle of the night and Toni wouldn't be there. I'd go looking for her, fighting away the aches and chills that were becoming more and more common between the hits, and would score for myself and wait for her to return. A feeling of desperation hung over us now as we begged for money, then hunted dealers.

When we couldn't find anyone at Tottenham Court Road, we would walk to King's Cross to buy heroin from the prostitutes. One pulled it out of her vagina, without caring if anyone saw. I didn't care either, I'd have walked to the end of the earth to make sure the withdrawal didn't last too long.

Heroin was everything to me, a faithful lover, my family and my dearest friend: nothing mattered when I was high. I was unaware of how my physical appearance was disintegrating,

The scabs that started off in my scalp were now all over my face and neck.

Months disappeared, a blur of friends' faces, coming round in Leicester Square, laughing to friends laughing at me, or concerned faces peering down at me – old faces disappearing, new faces arriving. Fights. Attacks. I would be talking to someone and gouch out, and come to thinking I'd nodded off for a minute, only to realise I was talking to someone else and half a day had passed. I found this funny. Sometimes I had no recollection of full days, my mind blanking out whatever happened so it wouldn't haunt me.

Patrick pops by after another long disappearance. The only people I have really spent any proper time with are Toni, the prostitutes we shoplift for, the drug dealers and passing hellos to Liam and Ben, who are completely lost in their own world too now. Our friendship group has shrunk drastically, and there are only a few of the hard-core drunks now hanging out in the park. London seems to be getting more grey and hard. The weather is turning to autumn, and the nights get colder. The city gets meaner.

Patrick is really upset with my appearance.

'What's going on with your face? Come on, kidder, you can do better than that. We need to get you to the clinic at The Connection, they'll be able to sort it out easily.'

I touch my face, my cheeks, my forehead and can feel the scabs that now cover it.

'Let's go for a walk, get something to eat.'

I look at Toni, who is fast asleep.

'Come on, leave her to sleep.'

Quietly climbing out of my sleeping bag, I walk with him in silence to McDonald's. I am high and embarrassed. I've been avoiding looking at my reflection as I don't recognise the girl looking back at me. I want to be scarred and grotesque, to keep men away from me. But the look on Patrick's face tells me it has gone too far.

I nip to the loo while he orders our food. My whole face, my hair, my neck, are covered in scabs. I've lost a tooth. I vaguely remember going to London Bridge training hospital to have it pulled out as it was sore, I haven't brushed my teeth in over six months. My reflection makes me want to take drugs. Patrick is sitting with our food in front of him when I get back upstairs. We sit in silence, eating. I keep nodding out, and when I shake my head to get myself together I notice Patrick watching me. He looks concerned. Sad. He just sits there, holding space.

'Come on, it's time to get the fuck out of Dodge, kidder. You're killing yourself. I've seen too many kids die around here. There must be someone I can call?'

I shake my head, not now, there isn't anyone I would want to see me like this. And I can't imagine not living with heroin.

'You know I was a crack addict for years? Probably about the same amount of years you've been on this planet. Five years clean. Look, I'm not perfect, I know I'm an alky, but that I can live with. I'm not robbing grannies anymore.'

He lifts up the sleeve of my hoodie and looks at my arm, dropping it when he sees the track marks. I nod off again.

His lecture is boring, anyone who questions what I am doing is boring. So I just let myself drift off.

'The Connection. The Connection. The Connection. I'm going to the walk-in tomorrow.'

'Come on, I'll walk you over now,' he replies.

I try to explain that Toni and I are going to get our own place, but I'm not sure it comes out clearly. In the end he gives up and says he has to get back to work. He drops me back to our spot and Toni is awake. I can see there is no love lost between them, she can't even be bothered to say hi to him.

'All right, kidder, you look after yourself, all right, you know where I am if you need anything.'

I can see him shaking his head as he walks away. I feel ashamed that I have let him down. But even that doesn't last. Soon I am back in my soft, black hole.

29

One morning I come round and feel different, for no reason.

It has come from nowhere, a real moment of clarity.

I want to clean myself up and go to The Connection to see a doctor about my scabs, wash my clothes and see if they have any new donated things.

I go to McDonald's to go to the loo to have a mini-wash. I remove my grandma's ring she gave me, the one my grandad proposed to her with, to clean my dirty, sore, scabbed face, and I forget to put it back on after. I only realise when I am halfway to The Connection and by the time I run back it is gone.

The doctor tells me I have impetigo and scabies. He gives me creams and a special pink soap to wash with and I stock up on new needles. I have a shower and use the things he prescribed and feel really headstrong about sorting myself out. I walk up Charing Cross Road and a mum is feeding pigeons with her young kids. I see instead my mum and my sisters.

Hovering around a phone box near Old Compton Street, I talk myself in and out of calling my mum. Will she be angry? Will she have me arrested, just to get me home? Or will she be upset that I have put her through all of this?

After a short while I decide to call; I want – no, need – to hear her voice. I feed some change into the payphone and dial her number. The pause. The sound of the number being typed in. Shit, it is ringing. She picks up.

'Hello?'

I can't speak, I freeze up . . . I can't breathe.

'Hello? . . . Lorna?'

I hang up, staring at my hand still wrapped around the receiver. The pale, dirty hand that now has tiny scabs and bruises across it. My veins are not holding up well and I am having to fight harder to find a vein when I shoot up. I've overused both arms and am now working my way through my right hand.

My trackmarks have sidetracked me. My mum. I should call her back. I want to call her back. Her voice fresh, it echoes in my head, 'Hello' . . . It was tinged with hope, but also with fear. Does she always answer the phone like this? Was she waiting for my call? Or waiting for a call from the police to say that I was dead? It sounded that way. I want to call her back, but something inside of me can't do it again.

I leave the phone box and decide to keep using the wash and cream. I will cut down on the drugs, then I'll call her once I've cleaned myself up.

More days pass. Or maybe it is weeks, I've lost count. This day of clarity is the last in a while.

I am sitting in my spot half begging, half nodding off, when a shadow looms over me. I open my eyes and see Seb, his curls longer, his eyes sparkling. He looks clean and full of energy. At first I think it is a dream – I've missed him so much. But he looks sad. Why is he sad? He puts his hand on my shoulder as he crouches down to my eye level. Then I realise it is because of me.

'Where have you been?' I cry.

'I got given a flat in Margate, but the town was full of junkies. It's a shit hole. So I'm back, getting myself in a hostel and saving up this time. Going to go back and study.'

He can't stop staring at my face. He squeezes my shoulder and gets back up.

'I can't stay, got to get some food and ring around the hostels to find somewhere, but hey, I'm going to get some leaflets on the different colleges, I'll get some for you.'

Whispering back, I tell him to come find me when he is sorted. I don't want this life anymore, I want to have energy again, I want to skip about and laugh and get drunk and be silly. I want to study, I want to be normal again, to have something to do with my days. To wear nice clothes and not be covered in scabs. But I don't think I could ever handle detoxing, or the reality of what I'd need to do. I would get arrested the minute I applied for a course, I'd never be allowed to just 'start again'. He leaves and I watch him walk away, consumed by my hopes, but controlled by my fears.

I drift off into a dribble state.

'Maybe I could? Yes, I could just study under a fake name, they would never know. I'd become the world's greatest artist and then I'd reveal myself, and the police would let me off because the prime minister would demand it. Yes, that's what I'll do.'

'You what? What you going on about?' Someone briefly interrupts my thoughts. It's Toni.

I laugh, embarrassed – I've started doing this more and more, lost between two worlds, speaking out loud. Sometimes I come to, laughing, and notice people's faces as they walk past me, giving me a wide berth. I pull myself up and shake myself awake.

I tell Toni about what Seb told me and that we should go to college too. We make a pact: we'll get clean and get a place to live and go back to school. Renewed in our excitement over our new plan, we sit on our steps across the road from each other and beg with excitement. We've planned one more wild night tonight, one last hurrah, then we'll get somewhere to stay so we can detox together.

'Fucking rehab,' Toni says. 'Look, it's fucking brutal, but I've done it before and we'll do it together, all right? The first three days are the worst, then it's the head you have to watch out for.'

We get enough to score and, unable to find any ampoules, we get some more smack from a dealer she knows. It is strong and I vomit right away, but it sends me into the beautiful, syrupy world I have lived for so long in. We laugh. We cuddle. We kiss. We roll in and out of consciousness.

30

The sound of police sirens drift into my dream – this isn't unusual. But then, the screams of the sirens become a man's urgent voice shaking us awake. Toni and I sit up with a jolt. It is Seb.

It isn't late, maybe midnight?

We are in the 'zone', but we can see the fear in his eyes.

He repeats himself, we have to get out. Liam and Ben, the Canadians, have been murdered. The police are arresting everyone.

None of what he says makes any sense. He pulls on our arms, trying to get us up. I tell him I saw them just earlier. I tell him they can't have been.

Toni also tells him to fuck off and go back to 'Pick-a-willy'.

But his eyes tell us it's real. He is scared and in shock, his face is white. No. They can't be . . . I get up and start to run towards their patch, Toni and Seb chase after me, shouting at me to stop.

I see police cars darting past me, leading me on. I run up Walker's Court and find that the police have cornered off Liam and Ben's patch. I can see blood, and feet. I know those feet. There's a lot of blood. I stumble. Seb holds me up. I see Toni staring. I try to get closer. A blanket is laid over their bodies, but I can still see the feet. They are Liam's feet. I am trying to get to them, to see if I can resuscitate them. Why isn't anyone trying? I feel people pulling at my arms and hoisting me away. It is as if someone has kicked my legs from under me. I can't walk or run.

31

I come round; I am in shock with the itches.

None of us say anything, we just stare into the nothingness.

Toni eventually stands up, declaring she needs a hit. Seb says he does too.

I have never seen Seb do smack, he has always seemed so against it, but we all squeeze into a small pay-per-use loo near Charing Cross and take it in turns to hit up. We go back to the park and curl up, exhausted and empty.

Who had done it? Why would anyone do that?

Every time I close my eyes, I see Liam's feet and the blood.

The sun eventually rises and the birds eventually sing.

The area is still cordoned off. I can see the stain of their blood on the floor. A drug dealer is also there with a dog; he puts his hand on Toni's shoulder and tells us to get out of here. Toni wipes her face with her sleeve. We follow him as he leads us to the Haymarket NCP car park. Not a word is uttered. When we get to the bottom of the fire escape he turns and hugs Toni. She melts into his arms and sobs. He tell us that Liam and Ben got into a fight with some guy outside a pub last night and that the guy had come back and killed them in their sleep. He turns to me and asks if I am all right. I nod but I can't feel my legs, something has split open inside me. He says he'll shout us if we want.

We all use the same needle. Toni between her toes, me on my good hand and him in his neck. I've never seen anyone shoot up in their neck before. He tells me to rest my head on his lap. I don't want to, but Toni looks at me with clear instruction, so I crawl over to him and lie back. He strokes my hair with his grubby hands. I close my eyes and try to enjoy the numbing feeling the drugs give me. Liam and Ben float in front of me – it is them, but on the first day that I met them. We must have been lying there for hours when the dealer shakes me awake as he has some business to attend to. He says he'll come find us later, then tries to kiss me. I pull back, I can't. He smiles and touches my cheek before walking away. As soon as he is out of earshot, Toni turns to me.

'You fucking idiot, are you trying to fuck everything up for us?'

Her energy shift is vicious, I'm not expecting it, this energetic punch in the gut.

'He's one of the good ones, and he'll look after us both. We'd never go without again if you're his.'

She shakes her head and gets up, pacing around angrily.

'You fucking shallow bitch, had you stopped to think that maybe he's the best guy out there, and you should think yourself lucky that someone is interested in you . . . Look at the fucking state of you.'

This cuts deep. I shrink smaller and smaller. I burn with embarrassment.

She's right.

She's right.

Maybe he is the best thing out there.

And he likes me.

32

On Toni's advice I let the dealer be my boyfriend, and find that if I get high enough I'll pass out and things don't seem to bother me as much.

I am 'his girl'.

He only comes by every couple of days, so I can handle it. But it leaves me feeling even more empty inside, the pretending, the desperation.

Patrick keeps coming by every day to check up on me with a sugary tea. Then one day he tells me that my picture has been in *The Big Issue* as a missing person, and that those dead parents of mine are looking for me. He stands there silently, waiting for an answer. But I have nothing to say, I can't fight it anymore. I don't care if he never wants to speak to me again. I just don't care. I am thinking a lot about dying, I can't see a way out of the cycle. When I am high it is fine, but those moments in between, I want to disappear, to overdose, I believe that that would be the best way to slip out of this existence. Patrick brings me back round with a shake . . . He tells me I should call my parents and let them know that I am still alive. He says he'll call them if I want. My eyes feel so heavy I can't keep them open.

'Come for a walk, let's get you moving and we can have a talk.'

'I can't, I need to get some money, I haven't eaten.'

'I'll get you something, come on.'

'But I'm not feeling well.'

He nods, he understands. I'm not going to go with him anywhere, I just want him to go so I can make my gear money and fuck off as soon as possible.

He sits down on the edge of my step and leans back, talking to me. It's as if he needs to hear it too.

'I never thought I would be able to kick the drugs when I was stuck on it. I mean, I always had these big plans, I was always going to just get it out of my system. It was always the dream, I'd go back to college, I would get my own place . . . I even applied to train as a carpenter once on one of those retraining schemes. But every time I lost someone out here I sunk further and further into the darkness. I'd be dead if it wasn't for this one person that didn't give up on me, that didn't walk away. Even when he wanted to. He'd been in the shitter, too, he knew what I was going through and never judged. He'd been to the depths, and he had come out the other side. And he helped me see that there was a life outside of all this.'

We sit in silence. I'm on edge and my leg is doing that crazy shaky thing. I feel worse than I've ever felt before, I need a hit with every fibre of my being.

Sensing what I am feeling, he gets up and squeezes my shoulder.

'It's OK to be upset about the boys, I'm heartbroken too. But don't let it destroy you. They wouldn't have wanted that.'

I try hard to keep my eyes open, but they are so heavy

that in the end I give up and just listen to him with my eyes shut.

'Come on, kidder. Things happen out here, and it just gets worse, never better. Time for you to get off these streets.'

I nod, hoping that if I agree he'll go, that he will leave as soon as possible. He looks at me with his big, sad eyes and backs away.

'I'll come check in on you later.'

Toni comes back with some cash, so we score, feed our seemingly eternal craving and everything feels full of colour again. We go to see who is in the park. The woman with the baby is already there, without her kid today, drinking with another drunk. They are rowdy, swigging from a bottle of vodka. Neither of them looks good. I ask where her little one is and she says her mum has taken full custody of it and starts ranting about how her whole family has conspired against her, but none of them 'fucking helped, none of them did a thing to help, just judged'.

She slurs about how she is going to get the baby back, get a job and a proper flat, she'll show them all. These are regular themes in a lot of the conversations – *we have been wronged, and they will be shown.* Haven't I even said this? Hearing these words come from someone else's mouth, I nod with understanding.

But still I can't help but feel that the best place for Karlie's baby is her mum's, until she does find whatever it is that she is looking for.

*

My heart skips a beat when I see Seb coming up the steps. I jump into his arms. He smells clean and looks really good.

'You didn't come back – you said you'd come find me.' I couldn't keep it in.

He hugs me tight.

'I had to stay away, I can't risk losing myself, that relapse scared the shit out of me. I'm back now, though. Fuck staying in hostels, no more fucking getting robbed. I'm over that shit. Anyway, Toni, let's go, I want to take you two out for lunch.'

We go to a cheap all-you-can-eat buffet where they sit us away from the proper customers. In the restaurant I can actually smell myself, I can smell my rotten unbrushed teeth as I talk. He tells us he has money and he's found somewhere new for us to stay, somewhere safe, away from all the crazies. He's changed his plan, he is going to work, save his money and get his own place, then apply to go to college next year. He takes out leaflets from his backpack on various courses and me and Toni look through them. I'm drawn to a BTEC one on Art and Design. Toni doesn't like the look of any of them.

'Fuck that shit – I don't need a piece of paper to do what I want to do. You guys can get lost in the system, but I'll be all right on my own, thank you very much.'

Seb winks at me and I smile – I love the way he holds space for Toni, doing it with humour. Never taking the piss out of her, always keeping it light. We finish up and I realise it is the first time I've eaten a proper meal in months. My stomach begins to hurt and I need to nod off. Seb says he has a surprise for us, and pays up, from a roll of £20 notes – I've never seen that much money before. He leads us through the Embankment park and to a raised level next to the river, under Waterloo Bridge.

'Wait here.'

He runs off ahead, swinging his backpack down from his shoulder, and rummages around to get something out as he disappears up the steps. We can hear him shuffling around and moving something that sounds like cardboard. Then I hear the clicking sound of his lighter. Is he having a smoke without us? I can see Toni thinking the same. We look at each other hungrily, but before we can charge up to see what he is doing, he comes bounding back down the steps and tells us to close our eyes.

Eyes tightly shut, we let him guide us both by our hands up the steps. It is a viewing area, overlooking the river – up ahead we can see the South Bank, and he points further up to the Houses of Parliament and Big Ben. He's lit a candle, and there is cardboard laid out in three spaces next to each other by the bench. Both Toni and I are speechless, it will give us shelter now that it is raining more, and it is far enough away from the madness of Soho. He takes some beer and crisps out of his bag and we lay out our sleeping bags, celebrating our new 'home'.

As it gets dark Seb says he has to go meet someone, so we all walk back to Soho, separating at Piccadilly Circus. Toni and I walk up to our begging patch.

'Do you fancy him? Seb? You know he hangs out all the time where we just left him? That's where all the rent boys pick up customers.'

I shake my head, no way. She's joked about it before, and I've heard her 'Pick-a-willy' insults.

'Where do you think he gets his money from?' She laughs, then pulls me back in for a side hug as we walk.

The evenings are getting cooler as the summer turns to autumn, and the turn in the weather seems to change the dynamic of the people we know. The younger ones seem to be disappearing, going elsewhere, leaving only the more drug-addicted, hard-core homeless around. We decide this is our last day on Shaftesbury Avenue. As the night slows down the dealer comes by. He sidles up next to me and kisses me. His front teeth are missing. Toni asks if he has anything, he looks at me as he says that he always has something for me. Toni jumps up excitedly. He puts his arm around me, and together we all walk to the car park as fast as we can.

As soon as it goes in, I know it is too much. I vomit, which I haven't done for a while, and as I breathe in I feel as if I am endlessly exhaling and my soul is slipping from my body. It feels like it is mixed with something, something I haven't tried before. I hear the dealer say something to Toni.

She is leaving.

I don't want her to leave me with him.

I can't call out.

A tongue in my mouth.

I try to pull myself up, weakly push him away.

I can't.

I hear him unbuckling his belt, saying something about how he is always giving.

I tell him I can't breathe.

33

A dark cloud comes over me.

Days pass, blurring and melting into one another. Memories play back through my consciousness until I take my medicine, then it all drifts away. I can't find the energy to leave our spot under the bridge. I tell Toni I'm sick, and she leaves me to beg and brings me food and smack. I lie cocooned in my sleeping bag, only getting out to go to the loo.

I get up and walk up the concrete steps across the road from us onto the top of Waterloo Bridge. I look down at the water, at the skyline of London. I look down at the drop to the water below. I want to fall. I want to fall endlessly. I scream out to London, but no one can hear me or wants to acknowledge me. Eventually I hear Seb's quiet steps coming up behind me.

'Want a fag?'

We stand by the wall looking out at the water. He asks if I am all right. I shake my head. He puts his arm around me and I rest my head on his shoulder.

'It's time to get away from all this.'

We give ourselves a month, we'll save everything. And he tells me straight up, as soon as we get away from here he's going to detox me and get me off this shit. Our talk calms me down and we walk back down the steps to our nest. I fall into a deep sleep, not waking until late in the afternoon the next day. And by then the dark cloud has begun to shift.

34

Toni has an idea, and jumps up.

'Follow me.'

We weave our way down to Waterloo Station, then hop over the barriers, just making the train before it pulls out. We find a quiet seating area at the back of the overground train. She won't look at me and just continues staring out the window at the passing scenery.

'Look, I'm going to borrow some money, but don't say anything when we're there, OK?' she eventually says.

The train heads west. I've never been anywhere in London other than Camden or Soho, and the train stops at places I've never heard of.

Further away from dealers. Further away from getting a hit.

We get off the train at Feltham. There are no barriers to jump, so we just walk out into the street. Toni is walking so fast I have to jog to keep up. We continue until we arrive at a small tree-lined street of pebble-dashed houses with manicured gardens and multicoloured hanging baskets framing each doorway.

She stops in her tracks, turns round to me and takes a deep breath before reminding me not to say anything and to let her do the talking. Then she grabs my hand and I follow behind her apprehensively. I've never seen her act this way before. She is about to press the doorbell, but then she turns to me again.

'God, you could have had a fucking wash, look at the state of you.'

She tries to smooth my hair down and then tucks in her T-shirt and pulls down the sleeves of her tracksuit jacket to cover up her arms. She spits on her sleeve and wipes my chin and cheeks. She forces a smile at me and then rings the doorbell.

No answer.

She walks into the front garden and looks through the living room window as a door opens inside. She quickly appears back at my side as the outer door opens, revealing a short, elderly lady with grey set hair, wearing trousers and a cardigan. The smell of baking yeast drifts out from the house. I notice a young boy, around five with a mop of blonde curly hair, peeking from behind the kitchen door. The kid has the same hair and wide mouth as Toni.

The old lady turns to the child.

'You go back inside, Harry, go finish your colouring.'

She watches him disappear through a door of the hallway, then steps out onto the doorstep, closing it slightly behind her. She looks at Toni with contempt and hisses in a hushed tone,

'What the hell are you doing here?'

'I just wanted to see Harry, that's not a crime, is it? You keep saying I don't care enough, well I'm here, aren't I? I've got a job now, we're getting a flat, aren't we, Tammy? And going back to college next year. Just wanted to come and tell you the good news. Come on, Nan.'

Her nan doesn't want to let us in and has her hand on the door frame.

Toni continues, 'Like I said, we just want to come in for a cup of tea and something to eat so I can see Harry, he's grown so much. Then we'll go and I'll invite you over once we're in our new place'.

The old lady seems to have heard it all before as she rolls her eyes and turns back into the house. She motions with her hand for us to come in, shaking her head.

'It's not right and it's not fair on Harry, you just popping up like this, then disappearing again.'

'It's different this time, Nan, I'm getting paid at the end of the month, so I'll be able to help out more. It's legit this time . . . I promise.'

We follow her through to the kitchen and she pulls out two chairs from the breakfast table before setting about making a pot of tea in silence. It's the first time I've been in someone's home for almost a year. Harry holds on to his nan's legs and stares at us both. Toni smiles at him, reaching forward and putting her arms out for a hug.

'Come give your mum a hug, little man.'

Mum.

Give your mum a hug.

It makes my chest feel tight.

Toni is a mum. And here is her child. She's never mentioned him before, or that she even has a kid. Why hasn't she told me? We tell each other everything.

He looks scared, like she is a stranger, and holds on to his nan's legs even tighter.

'He's confused Toni, he hasn't seen you since Christmas. Children need consistency,' says the nan.

Toni gets up and tries to pick him up, but he wiggles out of her arms and goes back to the nan's legs. Toni looks bruised but mostly pissed off. She leans against the kitchen surface, lost in her anger. I can hear her thoughts, the blaming of other people, the *I'll show 'ems*.

'So where are you living now?' her nan asks.

'We're staying in a hostel in Charing Cross, and we're on the council list for a flat, the next on the list actually.'

Her nan sighs and bring over the cups of tea as if she's heard this all before. She sits at the end of the table, and again, looking Toni dead in the eyes,

'What do you want, Toni? Why are you here?'

'I'm here to see Harry, aren't I?'

Her nan sips her tea before turning to me.

'You look like you should be in school, how old are you?'

My voice seems to disappear. 'Seventeen,' I mumble.

I need to itch my legs, but I am scared of giving the game up. Toni looks like she is also withdrawing – sweat on her forehead, coupled with that inability to keep still or focus. I look at the veins on her nan's hand as she clutches her cup of tea. Watch the blood pump around them.

Toni breaks the silence and asks if we can make some toast. Her nan nods and stares into her cup of tea – she is clearly angry. I watch the scene in front of me: her nan and Toni . . . Back and forth, trying to read the situation. Why are we here? What is Toni doing bringing me here?

The little boy appears again with a toy plane and sits by his nan's feet, making it fly by and wheeling it through the air. Toni puts some bread in the toaster and says she needs the loo. The clicking timer of the toaster acts as a metronome to the silent scene. Harry continues to play. The nan stares into her teacup.

'You need to get away from Toni, she doesn't mean to, but she will destroy you . . . She can't help herself,' she says. Then she looks up at me suddenly with the full force of her eyes.

We hear Toni's creaking footsteps from upstairs.

'She has her reasons for being the way she is, I give her that, her mum had her problems too, but that doesn't give her an excuse to keep destroying everything. We've tried so hard . . .'

The sound of a floorboard creaking directly above us makes her trail off. She looks over to a picture on her fridge.

I follow her gaze. It is a photo of Toni as a young child, around six. That wide smile is unmissable.

'She was such a good kid. But her mum wasn't well and made some bad choices.'

The toast pops up. I jump. Then Toni comes bursting through the door, she seems freshly agitated.

'Come on, we better get going, I only wanted to pop by and make sure you and Harry were all right . . . I'll come over next week and bring you a present, Harry . . . Would you like that?'

Harry smiles and nods. The nan looks confused.

'What about the toast?'

Toni nods as if she's only just remembered, goes over

and butters it, passes me a slice, then says we'd better go before we miss the next train. I get up and follow her to the door, giving the little boy a smile and wave as we walk out. He just stares at us in confusion. As we step through the door, though, the nan calls out,

'Toni, Toni . . .'

She catches up with us at the door and grabs Toni by the elbow, turning her round to face her.

'I know what you're up to, all this shit you were saying, and to Harry . . . Don't you ever, ever, come by again. I'll call the police next time.'

Toni pulls her elbow away from her nan's grip.

'I don't know what you're going on about. Come on Tammy, let's go.'

The door slams as we walk away. Toni is walking ahead so fast I can't catch up, winding back through the suburban roads. As soon as we get to the station entrance she goes straight to a cash machine. I see her take her nan's purse from her pocket, take out her card and withdraw £200.

I notice inside the wallet is a picture of a younger Toni holding baby Harry. She looks happy. She looks at him with love. She empties the wallet of cash and throws it in the bin.

35

That night, Seb stands up and tells us he is leaving London.

'What about our plan?' Toni looks panicked.

'It's all just fantasy while we're here, we have to get away to start again.'

'We can do all that here – we don't need to live somewhere else where we don't know anyone,' Toni argues back.

Seb is right, but Toni would never leave London. I never realised that before, but this city is part of the very fabric of her being. I watch her with much clearer eyes, now I can see how dirty, how skinny and how ragged she's become. I look down at my own dirty, black fingernails.

'What are you doing?' she turns to me.

'I'm going.'

She looks away for a bit, then looks back and says, 'OK, let's do it.'

She tells Seb that he should go ahead of us, though, and sort the place out, and we'll start cutting back on gear and join him once he gets somewhere sorted for us all. He argues that this isn't a good idea, we should all go together. But Toni says she and I need one last hit.

He packs his possessions and sleeping bag into his backpack, says he has to meet an old friend now and he'll write to us at The Connection to give us instructions of where to call once he's figured everything out. As he leaves we reiterate that we'll see him in Brighton in a few weeks. From our platform I watch him walk off along the Embankment until his figure dissolves.

The drugs are the only thing keeping Toni and me together; going without for one day is enough to drive me to insanity.

Toni disappears, but a few hours later she comes back to our patch and says she is taking me to a friend's. She has new clothes for us to put on. I follow her to the McDonald's on the Strand and she pulls out a school skirt and a vest; she tells me to wash myself in the sink and put them on. I ask where hers are. She tells me a photographer friend of hers is looking for models, she's done loads, so he needs new ones. He would pay 50 quid for pictures and always has good gear on him, too. I clean myself with hand soap and dry myself with paper towels.

She leads me through Soho to Rupert Street, then through a sex shop on Walker's Court and down to its basement. A guy greets her as if they are old friends, then looks at me. He takes my hand and tells me how beautiful I am. I feel flattered.

Toni says she wants to party. He puts some music on his stereo and starts to prepare something on the desk. I notice a sort of mini film set, like a small white bedroom with a hospital bed in the centre. Then I notice the film camera, a small home-video one. I look nervously to Toni, she puts her finger to her lips and mouths,

'It's all OK.'

He hands her a needle and he watches her, with evident disgust on his face, as she shoots up at the end of a line of dots on her groin. She drops back with the needle hanging from her skin and mumbles how fucking mind-blowing his cocktails are. I ask what it is, he says it is heaven, as he fixes himself up. They both sit hunched, heaving . . . when he looks up at me his eyes have changed, they are now black, soulless.

I know then I am in danger. I look at the door and think I could just run out, get on the train to Brighton and find Seb. But the guy crawls across the floor towards me, he pulls me up and sits me down on the metal hospital bed, then pushes my shoulders back until I am lying down. I look at Toni for help, but her eyes are closed and she is sprawled out on the sofa, deep in her high. I feel the prick of the needle between my toes. It's like dynamite, whatever it is. I vomit to the side and he strokes my back, saying something to me, but his voice is disconnected from his mouth, everything has fallen out of sync. I fall in and out of consciousness as he films himself raping me.

When I come to, Toni has gone. My feet are tied to the metal at the bottom of the bed. The man is asleep on the sofa. I panic, I can't control my shakes, but I don't want to wake him. I undo the ties and gather my clothes. Just as I'm about to open the door, I see the camera, I remember the flashing red light from last night. I check the back to take the tape, but it has already gone.

I've lived in fear of anyone I love seeing that tape ever since.

*

As soon as the cold air hits me, I run, I run for my life.

The tape. It's destroyed me. I can never study, I can never work, I can never have a normal life. I am bruised and sore. I notice bite marks on my arms. I want to scrub my skin with bleach. I want to scream and kick and bleed. I want to kill Toni. She planned this so I would never leave, never hope for a bigger, better life for myself. She made sure that my hope was obliterated.

The only thing that remains is to end it all. An overdose is the way to go. I try to go back to The Connection to get my clean clothes, but it is closed. I try to beg, but people avoid me. I eventually make enough money to get a hit but I can't find anyone that has any gear for me to buy. Eventually I find my 'boyfriend' down the alleyway on Tottenham Court Road. He only has methadone to sell, so I buy two little glass ampoules. Even he seems uninterested in me now, as he tells me he's got a new girlfriend. I cry as I storm through the streets, it feels like people are stepping aside to let me pass. I hop down the steps to the loos at the top of Carnaby Street, swing the door shut and, without even locking it behind me, fill up the syringe with as much substance as I can.

36

I am here in blackness, voices morph into beeping, discordant sounds.

In the darkness I can feel my body being hoisted by hands I can't see but feel . . .

Then I float back into the darkness.

I hear something metallic being put down . . . Is it cutlery? Did I fall asleep on the sofa at home and it's dinner time? Then I realise there's a beeping sound, too. Two people whispering and a tug between my legs. Then a sharp pain shooting up my leg, and cramp . . .

My eyes open and I see that I'm in a hospital, hooked up to bags of liquid and beeping machines. A catheter bag between my legs is being changed. I can't move my head because I have a tube inserted all the way down my throat. I want to cry for help – instead I manage a groan. The nurse notices I'm awake and strokes my forehead and tells me to relax, she'll get the doctor right away. What happened? I try my hardest to remember what happened. Where's my mum?

More nurses come to see me and soothe me. The tube is eventually removed from my throat. When they go to leave I realise that the curtains pulled all around my bed actually reveal that I'm in a ward. What ward, please someone tell me what happened? I catch sight of my bruised arms, at the needle scars and scabs all over my hands and body.

I remember. I remember everything. Where are my clothes? The only thing of mine I can see is my red PVC bomber jacket, nothing else. Then I hear voices approaching, talking in low whispers before the curtain is pulled back, revealing a doctor and a couple of medical students.

'Hello, good to see you awake, you gave us quite a scare.'

The students around this doctor take notes.

He continues, 'Do you know where you are?'

I shake my head.

'You've been asleep for two days, so we had to put a catheter in. A nurse will come and remove it soon. You're extremely lucky to have survived.'

Now I just want him to go. I just want to get out of here and find Toni. I want to go back to my bridge and fall asleep in the shadows.

'What's your name?'

Without thinking, I blurt out my real name. My feelings, my cravings appear from nowhere – not the same level of thirst, as they must have put me on some form of opiates. But the addiction is back, the madness, the excitement of the hunt, the taste when the needle goes in, the feeling of oblivion. I tell him I need to go, and try to get the tubes out of my arm.

He tells me he can help me, that he has people here that can work with me if I want to get off the drugs . . .

He turns back to the students and they take down their observations.

Once they finish scribbling their notes the doctor tells me that I should stay just a bit longer to make sure there isn't any lasting damage from the overdose. And that I should try and rest for now. He has kind eyes. I trust him. The minute I lie back down the heaviness of my eyes and body comes over me again.

A quieter world sucks me in.

I drift in and out of consciousness, I only hear snippets of what is going on around me, as if I'm not here. Something about the urine test showing that I have a high dependency, so it would be a gradual process . . . I remember these words when I come around again. I don't know how long I've been out but there's sound of the curtains being pulled open, and the murmur of several voices. I pull open my eyes. It's the doctor again and two new nurses. I'm confused, did I just blink and drift off, or have I been out for hours? I pull myself up to sitting to keep from drifting off again. Feeling on edge and cold. My jaw judders and I ask if they have extra blankets I could have.

The nurse tells the other nurse to go fetch me one.

The doctor asks again if there is anyone I would like them to call for me. I shake my head, no. How would I relate to anyone ever again? How could I ever make things right? How could I ever walk down my road, or in my home town, what would people say to me? It is overwhelming, I want to open up my chest and rip out my heart. I wish I had died. My hardness melts away and desperation floods over me. There is something about him that makes me talk; the toughness, the act of it disappears.

'I want my mum . . . I'm in so much trouble, I don't know

what to do and the police are looking for me, they want to put me in prison . . .'

I cry and cry. He sits on the edge of the bed and puts his hand on my shoulder.

'Everything is going to be all right. It will be hard, those first steps will be the hardest. Don't worry about the police for now, the most important thing right this moment is to get well. You have put your body through a lot.'

He gives me some paper and a pencil and asks if I want him to speak with my family. I scribble down my mum's number.

'I haven't spoken to her for so long.'

He nods his head. As he's leaving I ask where I am.

'London Bridge.'

He gives me a sad smile, then pulls the curtain shut.

I lie back. I instantly regret what I've just done. I panic, I want my clothes. I want Toni.

A kind nurse comes in and asks if it is OK to remove the catheter. She tells me to let her know when I have been able to pass urine naturally. I nod and she smiles before leaving. I look at the drip in my arm, peel off the sticky tape and slowly pull it out of the vein. I take the sticky pads off my chest and slide out of the bed.

I can see my trainers under the chair, I slide them over with my feet and pick one up, remembering I had stashed money in the inner sole a while back – I lift it up to check and it is still in there. I slip the trainers on, still in my hospital gown. I pull back the curtain and notice two young nurses talking at the reception desk. I walk over to them casually and ask where my clothes are. They look shocked to see me out of bed, the younger one's eyes drift to my arm where the drip should be. She says my clothes have been sent to the laundry and will be back later. She says it is really important I don't take the drip out, I have damaged myself pretty badly and it is feeding me medicine as well as nutrients. She says she'll get the doctor to come and see me as she leads me back to my curtained-off bed. And leaves.

My body feels weak, but I need to escape. I need to get out of here now. I put on my red bomber jacket and plan my exit through the gap in the curtain. I see some visitors leaving and decide to follow them closely. My legs feel heavy, like I am walking through treacle, each step sucks up my energy, but I keep walking down the hall and wait with them by the lift. When it arrives we all pile in, and that's when the visitors see me. They stare. The doors open and I leave first, walking as fast as I can. Seeing the bright morning daylight ahead through the double doors, I am able to run and I burst through them. I have no idea where I am, I just need to keep going. The cold breeze goes up my night gown; I'm in trainers, a backless gown and paper knickers. And the hunger hits me, I am driven by my thirst to forget, and to find Toni. I hate her, I am angry with her, but we need each other.

I walk and walk, not sure where I am going. People are staring at me but I am past caring. I am thirsty and weak. I ask a passer-by if they have some change, but they swerve around me looking at the floor. I see my reflection in a show window; I look so tiny, in the white and blue calf-length hospital gown, my hair sticking up. I look insane . . . what am I doing? I don't know what to do, I know I should go back to the hospital. A lady stops and puts her hand on my shoulder and the whole world slows down. I can feel the warmth of her hand, like her energy is radiating out of it and pulsing into my body. I stop crying and look at her. It was her kindness I could feel. I just stare at her.

'Are you OK? Do you want me to take you back to the hospital?'

I shake my head, tell her I am thirsty and I don't know where I am. I need to get back to my sister at Waterloo Bridge. She tells me to calm down, it is going to be all right. She takes me to a shop and buys me some water and a sandwich and gives me a fiver. She asks why I've left the hospital. I tell her there is nothing wrong with me. She looks at me with eyes begging me to go back. I thank her and leave. I look back over my shoulder and see her standing still, watching me go. I feel better after the sandwich, it wasn't as scary eating as I thought it would be, and I down all of the water in one go. Then I head towards the bridge.

I need to find Toni and give her one more chance. We'll get some gear and I'll convince her to go to Brighton this evening, we'll jump the barriers and start looking for Seb right away.

I walk along the river, crowds parting around me as I approach, little kids point me out to their parents, but I don't care, I am fixated on two things – scoring and Toni. I hit the South Bank, the book stalls. I'll come back here once I've found Toni and I'll get a book for Seb to surprise him, I think to myself. I jump up the steps to the path that leads over the bridge and walk alongside the honking traffic. I can see the end of the bridge, my legs feel heavy, like they have weights tied round my ankles. I need to get to the other side and try to break into a run but the end slides further and further away from me. I'm getting closer, why can't I run any faster? I stop, out of breath, and look over the side of the bridge. It's high tide, the water looks peaceful. Boats packed full of tourists with cameras pass underneath. I make it to the other side and skip down the stairs that lead straight under the bridge, I dodge traffic, run up the steps to our little platform and stop.

Toni's not there, but some of her stuff is bunched up in a corner. Two young boys are there instead, they must be around 15. They are sitting eating on top of their sleeping bags. They have also laid out books to read.

I ask them where Toni is. They look at each other, then back at me. Silence. They know something, I can tell. Silence hangs for an awkward beat. Then one pipes up,

'The blonde girl who was sleeping here?'

I nod.

'People are saying she's dead.'

The other continues, 'She OD'd. They found her with a needle in her arm in an underpass in Marylebone.'

One of the boys asks if I want to sit down, he pulls out a packet of biscuits and offers me one. I look down at my trainers and gown. I sit on the bench.

I ask again if they have seen her. They try to say it again, but slower this time . . .

'We arrived two days ago, and some of the older boys were looking out for us on the Strand. We met Toni at Charing Cross Station, and she'd been helping us out. She said we could share this spot with her.

'But yesterday everyone was saying she'd been found dead with a needle in her arm.

'She hasn't been back, and all her stuff is still here.

'So it must be true.'

I lie back on the bench and close my eyes . . .

A calmness comes over me. I can feel it. She's gone.

37

I look through Toni's backpack. I realise I've never seen the things she carried about with her before. Books – I'd never seen her read. Among her clothes, a picture of her boy. And folded up foils. I check to see if there's anything left on them. Nothing. I put on her jeans and T shirt then head to The Connection to find out if they have seen her. But when I arrive I spot my 'missing' poster behind the reception on the wall, and dash out.

A voice. One I haven't heard in a long time. From what now feels like a different lifetime.

'Hey.'

It's Macca. He doesn't look well.

He is struggling to keep his eyes open. The memory of the last night I was with him fractures my thoughts, I shut my eyes tight, trying to push it out.

'Where's Orla?'

He says she's been hit by a car and is in hospital.

'I heard about Toni. I'm sorry.'

I ask if he's got anything on him. He looks as if he needs the company as much as I do. I follow him to the Strand and we go down the stairs that lead to the underground loos, looking out for the cleaners before sneaking into a cubicle together. He chucks me a new needle still sealed,

I tell him I am fine and can share his, he looks up at me with droopy eyes.

'You are insane, you should never share needles, that's how you get the diseases that kill you.'

'What do you mean?'

'Have you been sharing needles?'

I've shared so many.

'You should get tested straight away. Have you ever heard of AIDS?'

I shake my head.

We go silent again while he cooks up and we take our medicine. The last thing I hear him say is that a lot of people are looking for me, he's seen my picture in *The Big Issue*.

A loud knock on the toilet doors brings us round. It is the toilet supervisor, he tells us if we don't come out he'll call the police. Macca gets his things together and slips out, avoiding the glare of the man who follows us out. Macca asks if I want to come hang out in the park with him. When I say I am going to find Toni, he takes me by the shoulders and squeezes them.

'Toni's dead. She's really dead.'

I push him away and walk off. He calls out after me. Everyone has left me.

Everyone is dying.

I walk up the Strand, tears streaming down my face. She is gone, she is really gone. I can feel it, I know it. I see my reflection in a shop window. Where is the cocky kid who ran away, so desperate to be liked, where has she gone?

I walk down the road and turn onto Waterloo Bridge, on top of what had been my roof, sheltering me from the rain, cocooning me and Toni safely for these past months. I stop by the handrail and look up the river. Then down at the dark water. It calls out to me. I climb over the railings and stand on the edge looking over the river, this ancient river. I close my eyes. I feel calm. I can hear concerned voices behind me on the bridge. I don't care.

38

I close my eyes and put my foot into the dark air before me and lean forward . . . My stomach is in my chest. I change my mind. But now I am falling, falling, falling, faster and faster than I have ever moved before.

I need to breathe, I want to live, I want to live, please, someone, anyone, help me. I try to clutch at something, I try to clutch at my life. It's out of my reach.

39

'Your poor mum, you know, she's sat by your side all night and morning, she only just popped out to get some air.' The nurse puts her hand on mine and looks me dead in the eye. 'Someone must be watching out for you. You're very lucky.'

A few minutes later, my mum comes into the room and wraps her arms around me, repeatedly telling me that everything is going to be all right now. And not to be scared. Just stay and everything will be all right. She tells me the police have been by and that she is supposed to call them as soon as I wake up, but the doctor says I need rest and have to stay for a few more days to heal and for observation anyway.

'I'm leaving soon, to move in with a friend in Brighton,' I say.

I am angry. I avoid her glare, but then she does something I'm not expecting. She puts her hand on my shoulder.

'It's OK, I'm not going anywhere, we'll get help; we'll get through this.'

She understands.

I don't want to go back to the streets, I want to go home. She holds me as I cry. She fills me in on the kids and that my big brother has a job now, and a girlfriend. Then she asks what the doctors have obviously told her they need to ask.

'Have you been sharing needles, or having unprotected sex?'

I nod. Yes. And yes.

The doctor comes in and my mum gives her a nod. She tells me she's just going to get a cup of tea and she will be back soon.

I tell the doctor everything: the needles, the drugs and all the other things that have happened to me, and hearing it out loud, coming out of my mouth, I realise I am totally detached from it all. They take blood tests and give me a full health screening. A nurse pops by to see me and we discuss the possibilities, she gives me leaflets and helpline numbers and explains that, whatever comes back, there is some incredible advanced medicine nowadays and not to be scared. They think, like I do, that I will have HIV.

I agree to go on a methadone programme, to try to start to wean myself off heroin.

I am in a weird no-man's land of being too young to be in rehab, but too old for the children's ward, so I am separated from the rest of the ward. When it rains on the hospital windows I worry about my friends who are still out on the streets. I miss the chaos. The hospital room is filled with too much silence. Too much sterility and routine. My mind, finally, has nowhere to escape.

The police told me what happened after I jumped. I had been pulled out and ferried back by staff at the Royal Lifeboat station, which was mercifully 100 metres from impact. That was the miracle that saved me. I had completely forgotten about that small floating office next to our under-the-bridge home. They told me they were going to take me back to Watford when I was well enough, as I had outstanding warrants for my arrest to deal with. But not to worry about that right now, and to focus instead on getting better.

They were kind – they told me they were just happy I was alive. These small acts of kindness were the difference between life and death right now. I had been so overwhelmed by the fear of what awaited me, of life without drugs, living instead with the memories and pain that invaded my thoughts. But the kindness of these two police officers made me feel that maybe there was still a life out there for me.

Early the next morning Mum brings some of my old clothes for me to leave the hospital in. They just hang off me now. I look at my reflection in the loo – my trousers hanging, my ribs showing and my bruised face and body. I tell my mum I want to come home, I want to start again, have a fresh start. I'm scared. But I'm ready.

'I don't know how, but we'll figure it out,' she says. 'Everything is going to be OK, I promise. And don't worry about the people on the estate, fuck them all, in a few weeks there will be something else for them to gossip about.'

40

As we pull up outside our house, I ask if we can just wait for a minute. I need to collect myself. She understands so we sit in silence. I look up the street. Who knows I am coming back? The green is empty, I can't see anyone. Maybe I can hide away forever.

'You ready?'

41

Weeks, months and years all blend into a fog, bashing and crashing into multiple lives, multiple friendship groups, careers, addictions. Alcohol, heroin, restricting food, abusive relationships. Starting over. And over. I read somewhere that a famous author would get up at 5am to write while the world was sleeping. In this sleepy world of 5am, my lives twist and merge into one.

In one life I am out with colleagues in an American diner. Post-film. I black out on drink and wander off, wake up in strange places, forced to piece together my night from the receipts I find in my pockets.

Another early morning, as an escort, a posh, young coked-up man stands back to get a better look at me; smiling, he calls for 'the boys'. The door opens and two of his friends come in wearing dressing gowns and big grins on their coked-up faces. They look at me like I am a giant cake they are about to demolish. There has been no mention of three.

'A filthy little whore like you should count yourself lucky that we'd even want to touch you.'

A filthy little whore.

I am not a 17-year-old with dreams.

To them I am just a dirty little whore. I want to scream,

shout, claw at them, but I can't. I just need to survive. I think of Sparky, of the *other* men.

I'm back at home and it's 5.30am. I dial the number she gave me. We fucked that morning like we had done all week. I loved her, she loved me. We were the same person but also two different women who lived by two different clocks. The clanking of my fingers on the phone's buttons stops. I wait. The static of the phone hums in my ear. Then a metallic voice: 'The number you have dialled has not been recognised, please hang up and try again.'

Six am in Homerton psychiatric hospital, I groggily awake to my wrists sewn back up and heavily sedated on medication. I told the paramedics that night that I wanted to die, and that everyone would be better off if I wasn't around.

I meet The Writer at 7am as I work as a stripper. He talks and talks about the films he is working on. At the end of the night he begs me for my number, and I break one of the cardinal rules: never meet up with clients outside of work.

At the strip club they ask if I'm pregnant, my breasts look 'soft'. I know in that instant that I am.

'How could you be so stupid? You'll be a sad, single, teenage stripper mum and no one will go anywhere near you', The Writer says before he hangs up.

My life as a mum starts in deathly pain. The nurses come over and tell me to be quiet, they say I'll scare the others on the ward. I tell them something is wrong, the pain is too much, I need them to help me. They laugh.

'What did you think would happen? This is labour.'

It's 9am, I have a very young baby in tow as I walk

through the door to the modelling agency. My new addiction, the monitoring and limiting of my food, is in full swing. I've studied books in the library on diets, they talk about foods I know nothing about – hummus, avocados, olives, wheat-free, gluten-free, rice cakes.

I'm in my late twenties, and I really am the last of my friends not to be earning money, or to have anything solid, and I'm still the only one with children. And I've even fucked that up. I should just get the train out of London, go to the woods . . . and hang myself. No one would miss me.

I finish writing a script by 10.13am and I say out loud, 'How dare you think of yourself as an artist? People would laugh if they read this . . . You are nothing.' I turn my experiences into a fable to process all the lives I have lived and draw them into one life.

It's 11.37am, I'm 31 and I have the itch to get smashed, the sweet, burned-caramel smell of heroin fills my senses, I am once more a vampire smelling blood on a wound.

The clock face drips and slides down the brick wall. Time hangs loosely around the ankles of my conscience. Things are going wrong, really, really wrong. I want to get a cab home, but I don't have any money, he's saying he'll get me home later. I want to go now. He's trying to kiss my neck. I'm going to be sick. He finally calls me a cab after he gets what he wants. I cry all the way home, spiralling again off into the vortex and confusion of heroin. Lying curled up, feeling warm and loved, where nothing hurts, nothing matters.

Two to three pm are visiting hours. My friends visit the detox centre, and cry, and judge me, and help me find things to be grateful for. I have a safe place, and friends, and a beautiful daughter who is safe. I want to write and make films. I have no major illness, and a whole world and life out there to do with as I choose. But still my body is finding the shocks to the system harder and harder to recover from. I have abscesses deep in my muscle tissue all over my thighs and back that I need operations on to remove. It is one of the most painful things I've had to deal with. And this little relapse made my thumbnails fall off.

My dad helps me unload an armchair at 3pm that I've managed to source on freecycle from his car and I lug it upstairs to my new flat in Swiss Cottage. The heating doesn't work and it's only a temporary loan from a friend in the US while he waits to sell it, but it's safe and it's mine for now, and I'm determined to make it into a haven for when my daughter visits. We spend weekend afternoons snuggled together in a cocoon in that armchair, watching films and sharing a bag of crisps.

Mid-afternoon, the third operation to sort out my drug-damaged body takes place. When I wake up, the darkest depression so far sets in. It's a chemical thing in my brain that nothing seems to shake. I try jogging around Primrose Hill in the mornings barefoot. I feel like I am drowning in a thick, dark liquid that is yanking my ankles under.

At 3.29pm, in another place altogether, I am given a second miracle, a baby boy.

I have a new life now, one with a kind and loving partner. I type up my thoughts and feelings and play around with ideas that are becoming more fully formed and unlock something creative in me. All the emotions that I blocked as a child come back. It's taken me a long time to learn how to be young.

It's late, I am behind the steering wheel of a man's car in Switzerland. I have stolen it so I can try and escape him. I am too drunk to take the turns and my focus can't keep up with the mountain paths. I swerve too heavily . . .

It's late. I am in front of my computer, why don't I write about a teenage runaway? Step back from it and observe it all as an outsider? Surely that would be therapeutic, too? To put it all into something, instead of carrying it around with me. I need to heal from my past experiences, to create, maybe to prove something to myself. Prove that I can do it right this time . . . I also need a reason to live, a reason to keep going.

It's too much. It's all painted there, pictures of what happened to me. I watch my time there, condensed, unfold, and it breaks me in two. I feel a mourning for the child I was. For the first time ever, I realise how young I was and how much has happened to me and not just in the scenes that I'm reading, but throughout my whole life.

When it gets dark, the newly resurrected memories haunt me like ghosts . . . I find myself breaking down for no reason in the queue for the food shop, on the bus a memory invades my thoughts and I have to put my head between my knees and slow my breathing down to stop myself from having a panic attack. All these lives are now part of me, they are part of my present, not my past. They have come back to life to possess me.

The more I sit in silence in the mornings, trying to focus on where these memories should go within my life, my art, the more I crave a drink. It starts as a treat, just once a day, with a rollie outside at the end of each day when the kids are in bed.

'My little treat.'

Brewer Street market, Soho, London.
June 2022.

I am invisible once more.

I'm standing on the corner of Brewer Street in Soho, watching as the world rushes at me. A churn of blurred faces, all with somewhere to go, in one of the few remaining areas of London that still feels dirty and dangerous. The area has been cleaned up; gentrification, they call it. But all you need to do is scratch at its surface and you will find the old world matted in its fibres. I can still spot the pickpockets up to the same old tricks. Sex still seeps out of the bricks and mortar.

It's early summer and tourists are starting to throng around Soho, brushing up against people on their way to meetings, important people on their big phones; walking into each other, not aware of the rest of the world filling these streets. A cacophony of sounds plays out across the scene: car horns, excited screams and police sirens. And then, that smell, always heightened by the summer heat: urine and garbage from the backstreets, along with hot coffee and food from the freshly sprung-up street vendors.

Almost all of the old brothels have been turned into fancy apartments. The massage parlours are now stark white minimalist art galleries. The age and filth of the old buildings stand alongside the glossy, newly built glass-fronted ones, which seem to have gone up overnight. At some point the old London will disappear, along with its generations of inhabitants.

But I can see what others don't. The ghost world which lies underneath the world of today, a parallel world, forever imprinted in time.

Standing by my side is a traumatised 15-year-old girl who is too scared to walk down this street in case she bumps into her past.

'You're all right, kidder,' a voice from a long time ago says to us both.

I hear the sound of an ambulance . . . a memory of feet and blood and police and sirens. I look to an empty doorway, it is there my two friends were murdered, in the doorway by the side of a Co-op. I can see their feet poking out from under a blanket. A pool of blood. Too much blood and death.

Someone in a rush knocks into me and scampers off without saying sorry – was that Toni?

As I walk down the road I see the shadow of someone I once knew huddled in each doorway. I walk past giant hotels which were once disused courtyards or car parks that I would spend hours in lost to heroin. Or take customers down to.

I pass a young homeless girl begging at the top of the stairs of Piccadilly Circus tube. She asks me for some change. My heart starts beating in my throat: that's where an Irish girl called Orla used to beg. She had long black hair and the most beautiful blue eyes you ever saw. She died after running in front of a car on a busy road while high. Macca's girlfriend.

I look away, pretending not to notice or hear her. I'll grab her a sandwich later and drop it round, I tell myself before moving off.

I keep walking till I arrive at a doorway with a gold plaque, it's the entrance to a private members' club. There is a line, albeit invisible. My legs start to buckle. So I sit. This used to be the fire exit of the tourist Italian restaurant, Bella Pasta. This is the doorway I slept in when I first arrived on the streets. The patch I'd beg at, too. I'm back down to street level, looking up at the passers-by, and sitting next to me is a kid who thinks she looks old, and tough. She looks to me like a scared, wide-eyed child.

My eyes fall onto the empty doorstep opposite. Where Toni used to beg. She smiles and waves at me, flashing a fresh £20 note she's just been given. A crowd passes between us and she is gone.

I move on to the car park. I duck under the same barrier and down the same fire-exit stairs. I can smell the same disinfectant, too. My head starts to pound, a sharp throbbing pain; the further down I go, the darker and thicker the air seems. This is where I would come. It still seems to be a popular spot: discarded bent cans and syringes litter the floor at the bottom and I'm sure I can smell crack in the air, like burning plastic. The light looks so beautiful, breaking through the metal staircase into tight slices on the concrete. I see Toni again, sitting there, on the bottom step, the scattered light flittering over her angelic face as she teaches me how to make a crack pipe out of a Coke can.

Back up to ground level, Piccadilly Circus is busier now, full of shoppers swinging bags and taking selfies. I decide to continue my walk through the city to Victoria, then get my train home. The train out of London to where I live never bores me. On a normal commute day, I spend the first half reading, then an internal timer goes off and I look up and out at the beautiful sprawling countryside, and every time I am filled with calm. I am safe. I've escaped.

But today's journey isn't like the other journeys. I can't concentrate or relax. Too fidgety to read, too tired to engage. I'm holding my hands in tight balls, digging my nails into my palms. I open them and stare at the demilune marks indented into the flesh. This is a feeling I haven't felt in a while. I used to get it, and I'd cut through my skin to bring me back into the present. I can't go there anymore, this time I have kids. I am their strength, they will learn how to interact with people and the world through me, and I'm never going to lie to them. The lies and shame for telling those lies, the hiding. I'm not doing it anymore. I try to breathe it away, my shoulders ache from the weight, and my chest feels like it's working on half capacity.

Stay present.

Breathe, Lorna, breathe. Focus on the trees outside the window whizzing past.

I want a drink.

Trees. Look at the blue sky.

I really want a drink.

I watch the strangers on the train instead. Taking in their details, studying them, trying to stay present. I notice a large vein on the side of a guy's neck. A warm feeling comes over me. I close my eyes and picture a needle slipping into a big throbbing vein on my arm. I taste it at the back of my throat, that tiny drip at the end of the needle, before I pull out my own blood and empty the syringe into my bloodstream.

Wake up.

Wake up.

I open my eyes.

The trees.

The sky . . .

Up until this moment being sober has been hard work, but doable. Seven years clean from heroin. Sometimes this cycle goes on for years. Sometimes it never ends. I've been getting sober, getting my life back together and destroying everything good in my life, on repeat for over 25 years. I think I must be on my fifth or sixth life now. Each phase is broken up by a relapse, and I'm exhausted with it; so are the people in my life.

Without allowing myself to think, I pick up a bottle of red wine from the shop across the road when I get off the train. I go home and greet my family with hugs and kisses, then get them to bed. And in the silence of the sleeping house, I treat myself to just one small glass of wine. Classy. Not like back in the day. I tell myself this isn't an addiction: this is a busy woman, on her way up, treating herself to a glass of wine. My friends and people at the 12-step meetings I've been attending don't need to know. Just one little glass of wine. I can be like everyone else.

*

Seven o'clock the next morning. I wake up to the pinks of my eyelids; the noise of birds tweeting and my head throbbing. I must have fallen asleep on the sofa. I slowly come around, too scared to open my eyes, so I curl up and try to go back to sleep. Then a memory. I sit up and open my eyes. Empty bottles by my side. I went out to get another bottle. My phone screen flashes on the floor. Another memory comes back – I'm filming my script burning on my phone. I look to the fireplace – ashes. Then I remember leaving voice notes to people I work with. I pick up my phone and check the messages. Several long ranty messages. Videos of me setting fire to my script, sent to the producers of my film, telling them I'm done. I remember trying to buy bitcoins. I look at my browser history.

That's right, I remember now. Bitcoin so I could buy methadone on the dark web.

I wanted some for the weekend, as a treat for when the kids were in bed.

You see, this is what it's like when I'm drinking. I'm not your average fun drunk, the one who has generic conversations, who is good at small talk and gossip – I take hostages. I tell strangers the deepest darkest secrets of my soul, I go home with strangers, leave my friends mid-night out and go on to nightclubs on my own, seeking more. I fall asleep in taxis or trains, set fire to scripts and send videos of it to the very people who hold my career in their hands. And instead of hangovers, laughing about the night before over fry-ups, I want to die. Not in the sense that most people do. I literally plan a way out.

My kids are waking up and I hear them sleepily walking to my bed to jump in with me. I can hear them coming down the stairs in search of me. I want to hide; I don't want to live this double life anymore. I don't want to lie anymore. I don't want to dance with death anymore. I've lost so many friends who have relapsed just for one night, but that one night was enough. I hide in the bathroom; I can't face anyone. Especially my kids. I sit on the loo for a while, unsure of what to do.

I don't want to waste my life dreaming of dying.

Afterword

Tuscany, Italy.
November 2024.

I wake up, once more, to a male voice telling me to *'wake up … wake up'*. I open my eyes and see the glow of my bedside clock, it's five to five in the morning. I turn over and see my husband sleeping softly beside me, one hand laid across me.

The voice I just heard – isn't his, it's a ghost voice. I've heard it before. I move out of our bed and walk downstairs to put on some coffee. The voice, it's so familiar yet I can't put my finger on who it belongs to. But, still, it comes back. Time after time.

This past spring, I married my best friend and we have combined families and now live in Tuscany. Life is tricky at times, and I still get things wrong but I'm the happiest I've ever been. I tell him that I spent the first chapters of my life running and the next chapters I want to spend dancing.

And as the years pass, my dreams of using heroin have lessened. My ability to step back when I'm overwhelmed is getting easier. And now my fear of my past being found out has disappeared I've learnt to acknowledge it has – and always will be – just there. In the past. Close enough to remember, far enough away not to touch.

And with that, I finally feel free. I know that one day death will come, but for now I want to hold it off for as long as I can; all of a sudden I feel like there is not enough time in the world. I don't dream of numbing these emotions anymore, I dream of dancing for the rest of my life side by side with them.

I know whose voice it is. The one that comes to me. I have always known.

'*Wake up. Wake up.*'

Acknowledgements

There are so many people to thank for helping me write this book. Many were not even part of the actual book itself, but without their love and unconditional support I would not even be here, let alone have written a book. Firstly, my mum, for teaching me you are never too old to educate yourself and build your dreams. My father for being a role model in how a man should behave, your childlike wonder still in your late sixties has inspired me never to get old. My siblings, you have all stepped up at different times over the years to help, love and support me, I love you.

Samantha Roddick for being the person that saw beyond my past and the shame I carried, which held me back for so much of my life and led to my repeated relapses as a drug addict. Sam set me off on my path to becoming a film-maker.

To Romilly Morgan, from Brazen, who held me and cheered me on through the whole process of writing this book, your unwavering support gave me confidence to keep going. Amy Sparks, without your support and belief in me none of this would have happened. Millie Hoskins, the most supportive book agent a girl could wish for. My wonderful editors and team Octopus: Pauline Bache and Caroline Taggart.

I need to thank all the genuinely gentle and caring men that I have met throughout my life, who helped turn my pain and distrust into warmth and taught me that men can be safe and supportive (without wanting anything in return!)

Peter Hellicar, you are the best father to our children that I could have ever have wished for. Thank you for teaching me how not to live only in survival mode. Ian Astbury, for offering me shelter when I found myself detoxing and homeless again as a single mum. Without this space and safety, I would not be here today. And without Ian, *Amà*, my first film, would never have happened. Colin Firth and Ged Doherty for believing in me as a writer when no one else did (including myself).

To those who held me up when I lived in poverty, lending me money, emotionally holding me and always helping me out, there are too many to mention here, but Andrea Vecchiato – you have secured your special place in the heavens. My children Georgia, Buddy and Lola – you have taught me patience, and how to love. Georgia, I am sorry that I knew nothing of how to mother when I had you, and I am so proud of who you are and have become.

To my husband Seamus McGarvey, for allowing me to be me, even at my absolute messiest, and loving me through it all. It took us 15 years to get it together, but you have changed the way I look at the world.

Endless love to Phoebe, Stella and Sam, for inspiring me with your very being and for welcoming me into your family.

To Karlie, Hermoine, Kirsten, Kat, Lorenna, Jemima and Tanya – you all rock and I love you so. Thank you for being the best friends a girl could wish for, and for not letting me push you away.

And to everyone that is still standing by my side throughout it all over the years, thank you.

About the Author

Lorna Tucker is an artist, writer and filmmaker, who has secured her place as one of the most exciting documentary directors working today, known for tackling big social themes with humour, ease and grace.

Her first feature documentary, *Westwood: Punk, Icon, Activist*, was an Official Selection at Sundance 2018. Her subsequent documentaries include: *Amá*, about the sterilisation abuse of Native American women over the past 60 years; *Someone's Daughter, Someone's Son*, chronicling stories of homelessness in the UK; and *Call Me Kate*, about the inner life of screen legend Katharine Hepburn.

She was named one of the biggest breakout female filmmakers by *Harper's Bazaar* and *Elle* in 2018, and one of Creative England's CE50 the following year.

She has written articles for *British Vogue* and The *Guardian*. *Bare* is her first book.

This **brazen** book was created by
Publisher: Romilly Morgan
Senior Developmental Editor: Pauline Bache
Editorial Assistant: Elise Solberg
Creative Director: Mel Four
Copy-editor: Caroline Taggart
Typesetter: Jouve
Production Controller: Sarah Parry
Sales: Sammy Luton and Isobel Smith
Publicity & Marketing: Charlotte Sanders and Ailie Springall
Legal: Nicola Thatcher